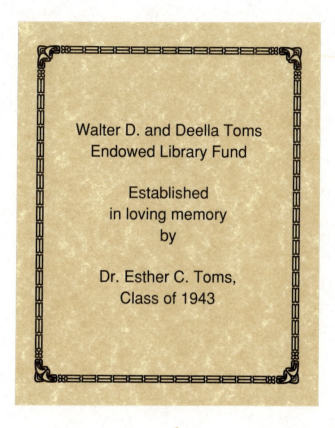

Writing Management:

Organization Theory as a Literary Genre

BARBARA CZARNIAWSKA

OXFORD
UNIVERSITY PRESS

OXFORD
UNIVERSITY PRESS

Great Clarendon Street, Oxford OX2 6DP

Oxford University Press is a department of the University of Oxford.
It furthers the University's objective of excellence in research, scholarship,
and education by publishing worldwide in

Oxford New York

Athens Auckland Bangkok Bogotá Buenos Aires Calcutta
Cape Town Chennai Dar es Salaam Delhi Florence Hong Kong Istanbul
Karachi Kuala Lumpur Madrid Melbourne Mexico City Mumbai
Nairobi Paris São Paulo Singapore Taipei Tokyo Toronto Warsaw

with associated companies in Berlin Ibadan

Oxford is a registered trade mark of Oxford University Press
in the UK and in certain other countries

Published in the United States
by Oxford University Press Inc., New York

© Barbara Czarniawska 1999

British Library Cataloguing in Publication Data

Data available

Library of Congress Cataloging in Publication Data

Czarniawska-Joerges, Barbara.
Writing management: organization theory as a literary genre/
Barbara Czarniawska.
p. cm.
Includes bibliographical references (p.) and index.
1. Organizational behavior. 2. Communication in organizations. 3.
Authorship. 4. Literary form. I. Title.
HD58.7.C933 1999 658.4'53—dc21 99-31593
ISBN 0–19–829613–4
ISBN 0–19–829614–2 (pbk.)

1 3 5 7 9 10 8 6 4 2

Typeset in Jansen Text
by Cambrian Typesetters, Frimley, Surrey
Printed in Great Britain
on acid-free paper by
Printed and bound in Great Britain by
Biddles Ltd, Guildford and King's Lynn

ACKNOWLEDGEMENTS

I would like to express my thanks to Mary Jo Hatch, John W. Meyer, and Lloyd E. Sandelands for their comments on the text.

Chapter 3 is a revised version of an article that appeared under the same title in *Organization*, 4/1 (1997), 7–30. I thank Sage Publications Ltd. for the permission to reprint it.

Chapter 6 is a revised version of an article that was published in *Studies in Cultures, Organizations and Societies*, 5/1 (1999), 13–41. I thank Harwood Academic Publishers for the permission to reprint it.

CONTENTS

Above the blank page lurking, set to spring,
are letters that may compose themselves all wrong,
besieging sentences
from which there is no rescue.

(Wislawa Szymborska, *The Joy of Writing*)

1

Management and Organization: A Field, a Theory, a Practice, and a Genre

Each practice has its own theory: thus management practice has its theory, usually of a normative character. An academic practice differs from others in that it has a theory of its own practice, and a theory of another practice, in this case, management. A theory of the academic practice, of which this book is an example, also has a normative character, although in this text the meaning of 'norm' emphasizes 'the usual' rather than 'the ideal'. In other words, I am not concerned with the a priori criteria of 'good' or 'bad' writing on management, although I assume that good writing is desirable to the readers as much as to the writers. Such criteria are, however, constantly constructed in specific times and places, and could therefore only be described a posteriori, together with a reflection on their emergence.

While there exist many texts occupied with the creation of management and organization theory in terms of methodology (a seminal work in this respect is Burrell and Morgan 1979), not much is said about writing management and organization theory (with recent exceptions being Golden-Biddle and Locke 1997, and a special issue of *Studies in Cultures, Organizations and Societies*, 5/1 (1999), edited by Steve Linstead). In this respect, management as a subdiscipline of social studies is lagging far behind economics (McCloskey 1986), sociology (Brown 1987; Van Maanen 1988; Agger 1990; Capetti 1995) or anthropology (Clifford and Marcus 1986; Geertz 1988). This is most likely due to the fact that management, or business administration, as a relatively new university discipline, still feels allegiance to the eighteenth-century ideals of (natural) science, which assumed writing to be the domain of literature and not of science (albeit producing copious writings on the subject):

Writing is an unfortunate necessity; what is really wanted is to show, to demonstrate, to point out, to exhibit, to make one's interlocutor stand at gaze before the world . . . In a mature science, the words in which the investigator 'writes up' his results should be as few and as transparent as possible. (Rorty 1982: 94)

The realization that writing is the organization researchers' main activity seems to be growing, together with reflection upon how they write and what textual devices they use, or could be using, in writing. But this reflection is neither easy nor obvious. Management, as a young academic discipline, is not yet prone to disciplinary reflection. There are even some difficulties as to what discipline it is to begin with.

A FEW WORDS ON SEMANTIC SEDIMENTS

The safest route for somebody undertaking a disciplinary reflection is probably via direct experience. Thus let me begin with what I know best—that is, my own job. I happen to be a professor in *företagsekonomi*, which should translate into English as 'Business Economics', but it does not. It has usually been translated as 'Business Administration' but recently, as a result of some inconsistencies between this umbrella-like name and its subdisciplines, has increasingly been translated as 'Management' (for more detailed analysis, see Engwall 1992).

There are at least two reasons for these mistranslations. A historical one has to do with a wish to indicate the end of German influence, traditionally very strong in the Swedish system of higher education, and the beginning of the US influence. Another, emerging reason had to do with the fact that, with the exception of business finance, most of the *företagsekonomiska* subdisciplines use organization theory and not economic theory as their theoretical basis.

As to subdisciplines, they may vary from one Swedish university to another, but the standard offer would be accounting, marketing, public administration (thus trouble with 'business administration' as the main subject; recently it has been called 'public management'), international business, and . . . organization. The latter had replaced the earlier 'administration', reflecting more general changes in the field (the 1960s shift from 'administration theory' to 'organization theory'), but creating havoc at the juncture between theory and practice. The original 'administration' dealt basically with personnel problems. As the present 'organization' deals mostly with theory, 'personnel' has left our departments and found refuge in Education, Sociology, or Applied Psychology Departments. Hence it is quite often that a specialist in organization theory holds the general chair and his or her speciality is not well represented at the level of applications.

This is a taste of Swedish academia: had I wanted to extend this disciplinary map to the USA or the UK, not to mention France and Germany, innumerable intricacies would emerge. I would have to account for Organizational Behaviour and Organization Development, HRM and Industrial Relations, Financial Accounting and Management Accounting, and so on and so forth.

While such a historico-geographical approach is undoubtedly needed and valuable, I will choose another route. The protagonist of this chapter is management and organization theory (treated here as one subject[1]) and its applications. The fact that such a discipline does not nominally exist, and appears in the academic surroundings under a variety of institutional guises, is nothing more than an indication of its evolution and transformation.

IS MANAGEMENT THEORY A PRACTICAL SUBJECT?

When, around the beginning of the twentieth century, our forefathers (plus Mary Follet) began forming the subject that later acquired a variety of names, they did so on the promise to solve any problems companies and administrative organizations might possibly have. Later, this role of 'company doctor' was further developed, especially by the Tavistock Institute, which was given large sums of money by the British government to help all companies facing trouble in post-war Great Britain (see e.g. Jaques 1951). At the same time, however, this kind of knowledge was becoming a strictly academic subject, with Ph.Ds and professors, refereed journals and international conferences.

Where are we now? Is ours a practical subject, which produces practitioners and improves practice? Or is it an academic discipline eager to remain in close contact with practice, with the purpose not of dictating the order of things, but of *reflecting and provoking* via basic research and theory? After all, is it not a strange idea that researchers from outside an organization can tell practitioners how to run their companies and how to be better managers; that these 'experts' are expected to reform and reorganize living organizations? Common sense would suggest that it is so. After all, if researchers are so good at organizational action, one might well ask why they are wasting their talents on academia.[2] And yet this assumption has persisted since the birth of this discipline. Researchers arrive, and, like car mechanics or physicians, they examine the 'body' of the organization, make a diagnosis, and prescribe a 'cure'. The discipline had, after all, made an oath to its practical utility. Does it still hold?

When Plato laid the foundations for Western philosophy (which have only recently been deconstructed), he promised the Athenian politicians to solve all problems that might arise: from guidelines as to how to conquer Sparta to methods for raising one's sons (Plato cannot, I am sorry to say, be accused of having been a feminist). When Durkheim laid the foundations for modern sociology, he promised to solve any problem French society might have: from German neighbors to poverty and crime. Both disciplines have ended up at an advanced theoretical stage, while the practical problems have multiplied, if anything. Should we conclude that all those promises were hypocritical, made with the intention of justifying oneself to society on false premisses?

---

[1] There exist organization studies that do not concern themselves with management, but I hope that most of what I have to say can be applied to these as well.

[2] In the same vein McCloskey (1990*a*) asks economists, 'If you are so smart, why aren't you rich?'

Indeed they were a means of justification. Those promises were, however, born not out of hypocrisy but out of enthusiasm and naïvety, so typical of the coming into existence of new ways of thinking. A similar contemporary development can be quoted here: that of environmental science, this new interdisciplinary subject asserting itself by promises of salvation. Yet, every acute observer of miscellaneous modernist projects is able to predict straightaway that this promise will not be kept. It is not that disaster is inevitable, but that, in order to stop it, a coordinated effort of a political, economic, and social nature is required. The task of environmental research is perhaps not primarily to solve problems but to bring them to light (Wolff 1998).

That which was once enthusiasm and exalted optimism, with time turns into frustration if things go wrong, and wisdom if things go right. Things have gone rather well for business and management sciences, which means that we are now in the position to afford some reflection upon *what* we are doing and *why*. If we are a practical subject devoid of intellectual ambition, then it is time to stop wasting society's funds: back to schools of commerce and to two-month correspondence courses in accounting and business techniques. If we are an academic discipline, however, we must ask ourselves what could be our contribution to the general debate concerning the desired shape of our society in the twenty-first century.

Contrary to appearances, we have much to contribute. However often we weep over the lost civil society, it is clear that such a society can exist only as a parallel to organized society. Without understanding much of it, we have become organized through and through (or, as Perrow (1991) calls it, we have become 'a society of organizations') and even those who are against organizations as such organize to protest against them. This is where the very duties and possibilities of organization science lie: in a theory of organizational society, with economics and politics seen as the two main forces of construction of that which constitutes society. There are no individual consumers or producers: they all watch the same television and read the same newspaper (in Sweden, in two main versions). The last of the individual producers and consumers was a quaint German living in Lapland, living off nature and help (returned) from neighbors. The Swedish immigration authorities have done all that was in their power to get rid of him.

What legitimacy do we have, what kind of theory can we offer, what status will the knowledge so produced have, and of what practical use might it be? Let us have a look at each of those issues.

THE EMERGENCE OF BUSINESS ADMINISTRATION

In 1935, in the USA, Thurman Arnold, a Yale lawyer who served as the Chairman of the Antitrust Commission, wrote an amazing book, called *The Symbols of Government* (where 'government' stands for 'governance' and not for the state authority), presenting an unusual view of reality, which, surprisingly enough, can easily be transferred from the USA in the time of the Depression to, let us say, Sweden of the 1980s (a feat accomplished by Brunsson 1985; 1989).[3] Arnold depicted society as composed of the subsystem of norms, values, and ideologies (including religion and science) where ideals went hand in hand with formal logic, and then the subsystem of practice—meaning mostly business practice—messy but effective. Most of the time in opposition, they were nevertheless connected to each other. The official version of this connection was that the world of norms dictated the rules to the world of practice. In Arnold's version, however, it was rather more likely that the world of norms legitimized practice as it went along, cleaning out some of its indecencies as required. Of course, such a liaison was neither simple nor unproblematic. There were whole gray zones of problems, and business administration, he claimed, just filled one proudly:

The ways of thinking of the business world have, of late years, also demanded scholarly recognition. Business schools have become an accepted adjunct to great universities. Again, that way of thinking which demanded logical arrangement and preconceived fundamental principles, compelled the professors of the business habits of the time to call their subject a 'science.' The 'science of business administration' has a congenial sound to the scholarly ear, and indicates that so far as possible it will avoid creating a mere 'trade school.' More freely translated it means that, in deference to scholarly thought, it will avoid studying business as it is, to study it as it ought to be, since the close examination of living institution is the enemy of all logical classification. Yet the business-school professors were so close to life that the best ones refused to become sufficiently theoretical to avoid academic suspicion that they were tradesmen rather than scholars.   (Arnold, 1935: 89–90).

There are many interesting threads to pick up in this opinionated utterance. It is of relevance here, because it contains all the problems that will be typical of business and management sciences during the first half of the twentieth century: being 'adjunct' to universities, even if accepted and sometimes (in times of prosperity) envied; being exposed to the 'scholarly' expectations that are never properly met; and having some members of the profession who rebel and refuse to be 'scholarly', choosing to be faithful to their 'practical' vocation. I believe that many of these problems can now be solved, when the notion of 'science' and 'theory' is redefined, and I will return to it in later sections. For the time being, though, let us look at Arnold's utterance as related to its historical context.

It is hard to say whom Arnold meant when he spoke about those who adapt and those who rebel against scholarly demands, but it is appropriate and instructive to focus attention on Chester Barnard as a symptomatic personage

---

[3] This section has no ambitions of presenting a complete historical narrative, which would have to start with Babbage in England, continue with Taylor in USA, Fayol in France, and Mayo in USA again. It takes up a specific aspect—legitimation—of organization theory within the discipline of business administration. For historical analyses of US management science, see O'Connor (1996) and Shenhav (1999).

of those times. As the practitioner he was, he decided to share his experience with all who needed it. To this end, he wrote a book *The Functions of the Executive* (1938). This classic attracted academic attention again fifty years later, when Oliver Williamson was entrusted with organizing a series of lectures at Stanford University in honor of Barnard, which resulted in a book of essays edited by him (Williamson 1988).[4] In this collection, various authors point out two interesting characteristics of Barnard's book. To begin with, his was no Iacocca story: Barnard put his experience into a highly abstract form, typical of the then legitimate social theory, so that even the most enlightened minds of our times admit they had trouble dealing with his dense and formal text. The second interesting observation is that this classic of organization science represents all that business and management sciences are *not* supposed to be: not only is this an abstract theory, but it is also arrived at through *speculation*, and not through empirical study. There is no doubt that Barnard wrote on the basis of his experience, but so did all the speculative theorists, from Plato through Thomas Aquinas to Immanuel Kant.

This was not, however, the meaning of theory as understood in the 1940s and the 1950s.

'THERE IS NOTHING SO PRACTICAL'

'There is nothing so practical as a good theory,' said Kurt Lewin, on emigrating to the USA to do research on democratic leadership (Lewin *et al.* 1939), and on the force of persuasion and on group dynamics in general (Lewin 1953). Lloyd Sandelands (1990) decided to take a closer look at that famous statement to see what implications it might have for organization science. His reasoning turned historical: there were at least three different interpretations of the famous dictum and they seemed to mirror a transformed way of thinking.

Apparently, Lewin himself wanted to build a bridge between theory and practice using experimentation. To him, theory was an idea that had to be tested: using practice, one would find out if the idea held or, if not, what was wrong with it. Even if this may sound convincing and rather practical, it is impossible, claims Sandelands. Since theories are formulated in a completely different language from action plans, they must first be translated into such plans. This could be done by researchers (who would then behave as practitioners) or by the practitioners themselves. But it is not theory that they would be using; they would merely be inspired by theory in their construction of action plans. In the same way, one may be inspired by nature or by a work of art. The aim of theory is reflection; the aim of action plans is action.

The developments in the social sciences brought more and more complications to Lewin's original statement. To begin with, it has been pointed out that

---

[4]   For a more deconstructive reading of Barnard's book, see O'Connor (1996).

experiments rarely, if ever, verify or falsify a theory. Even in natural sciences replications bring more problems than solutions (Latour 1988*a*). To continue, there are serious doubts about the transferability of laboratory experiment results to any other kind of social reality. It is not that the laboratory is 'unreal' or that reality is 'out there'. It is simply that laboratory reality is a reality *per se* that may or may not have traits in common with other realities. These doubts were deepened by the critique of the correspondence theory of truth (Rorty 1980) and, as a consequence, the idea of 'representation' (one situation standing for another) came into question.

But testing was not the only way to join theory and practice. Another way was, as it were, to 'theorize' practice. After all, plans of action are based on certain—tacit or verbalized—action theories. And, since practitioners construct their own theories of action, researchers should be able to come up with competing ('better') theories, as well as with meta-theories—that is, theories about the practitioners' action theories (Argyris and Schön 1974). Sandelands (1990), however, pointed out that this leads to the creation of an additional problem rather than the solution of the original one. When it comes to practice, people are not conscious of the action theories they are applying. Everyday theories are much more incomplete and intuitive of character than are academic ones. If one asks successful entrepreneurs how they go about things, the answer is often a set of platitudes that are at best trivial and at worst quite evidently false. Do they not know what they are doing? Not exactly, nor do they have to. One does not need a diploma from a school of engineering to be able to drive a car.[5] What is more, it is highly improbable that researchers should be able to come up with a better theory of action than do practitioners, unless they become practitioners themselves.

Instead of simplifying our dilemma, Argyris and Schön complicated it even further. Yes, practitioners do have action theories, which, albeit different in content, are quite similar to scientific theories in form, which means that they are made of different stuff (or, to put it more elegantly, belong to another sphere of discourse) from practical knowledge. So, now we have to interpret first actions, then action theories, then the relationship between the two, then scientific theories, and the relationship between the two types of theory and practice.

Does it mean that research and researchers have nothing else to offer to the practitioner but the typical academic hair-splitting? They have much to offer, but within their special area of competence and not in competition with the practitioners themselves. The social sciences are a system of institutionalized reflection, whereas business and public organizations represent institutionalized action. It is obvious that the two are different and separate, but it is equally obvious that they have much to offer one another. Action is the subject of the

---

[5] The irony of events would have Milton Friedman use the same argument to a dramatically different purpose: he says that people are able to use the results of theoretical (economic) reasoning without understanding it (Friedman 1953).

researchers' reflection; reflection offers to action the possibility of change and renewal. The two together—starting with the notions of 'action research' and 'the reflective practitioner' (Schön 1983)—have ultimately become institution-alized in the consulting profession, which mediates between the two worlds but which also strives for a special competence of its own, based on just this unusual combination of action and reflection.

But let us proceed to Sandelands's third interpretation, which treats theory as a kind of practice. The product of theoretical thinking is tropes, or rhet-orical figures (see Morgan 1986), which, though still not connected to practice, can provide practice with new inspiration and evoke interesting associations, just as art does. Tropes such as 'garbage can', 'bounded rationality', or 'muddling through' entered the practitioners' vocabulary with no need for formal schooling in works that produced them.

This is, in a sense, an opposite solution to the previous one. While action theory theorizes practice, this approach 'practices' theory. Consequently, research and education within business administration are a practice in its own right, with its own rules and its own action theories. Its product is *theory and reflection* (or, in the case of students, the habit of reflection). As a conse-quence of this, the relationship between organizing processes in a company and organization science in academia can also be redefined. The contact between the two has to be close precisely because it becomes increasingly evident that ours is a discipline that is inspirational. An academic discipline, when isolated from practice, becomes dull and self-centered. Practice without reflection becomes routine and repetitive. As theoreticians, we should be telling practitioners about what they could never come to think of themselves, and not about what they know already and better.

All these solutions are of great insight and value, and all are applied to a great many situations. Still, the chasm between theory and practice gapes as wide as ever, says Sandelands (1990), causing quite a few legitimacy problems (see Astley and Zammuto 1992). At this juncture two observations must be made. One is that, when speaking about theory, Sandelands had in mind a specific type of theory (which I shall call a 'logico-scientific' one); the other is that, while speaking about practice, he concentrated on tacit knowledge, no doubt of central importance to practice. There are, however, other types of theories and other types of practical knowledge.

PROBLEMS AND SOLUTIONS REDEFINED

The recent way of thinking about theory and practice and the relationship between the two tends to redefine the problem. First of all, the critique of the correspondence theory of truth (Rorty 1980) brought us the understanding that theory, belonging to the domain of language, cannot 'represent' reality in any iconic sense. Events do not unfold in a logical sequence; only sentences do.

Thus it has become clear that field research is not an 'imitation' of practice and theory is not its 'reflection'. Accordingly, Brunsson (1982) postulated that the main role of business and management science as a discipline is to furnish a language of description (I would say interpretation) and reflection to practitioners and theoreticians alike. The concepts of 'science', 'knowledge', and 'theory' are changing, and making room for new meanings.

This change was accelerated by the 'postmodern revolution'. The idea that scientists should be out improving reality was all a part of the Modern Project, claimed Lyotard (1979/1987). This project, whose roots lie far back in time but which came to fruition in the twentieth century, was characterized by an extreme arrogance masked as a program of emancipation. It was arrogant towards nature, which was to be controlled and exploited by humans, and it was arrogant towards those doomed to the need of emancipation, such as developing nations, workers, women, and children (Mitchell 1987). A logical part of this view was the superordinate value assigned to science, which replaced religion, thus endowing scientists with a privileged status.

What research has to offer now is not emancipation, but freedom from old versions of social reality (Rorty 1992a). Rorty agrees with Lyotard that we should give up the ambition to emancipate other people, because such a program always conceals an arrogant assumption of superiority and 'knowing better'. But this does not mean that we cannot try to convince other people that many versions of the world are possible, and, rather than criticizing their versions, we can try to persuade them of the attractiveness of our own.

In the specific case of organization theory, the task of the researcher, as I see it, is to free practitioners from the 'iron cage'—from the trap that the world they have constructed for themselves has become for them. By convincing them that it does not exist 'out there' objectively and immutably, but that it is constructed by people in a joint effort, the researcher can also persuade them that other constructions are possible. But the decision to change and the choice of alternatives are in the hands of the practitioners (and always have been, modern ambitions notwithstanding). It is perfectly legitimate for them to say: 'Now we are convinced that we are the constructors of the world we live in, but we still like the way it is, thank you.' But by showing practitioners some of the unexpected aspects of what is regarded as self-evident in organizations, researchers provide an opportunity for shared reflection, for thoughts that might lead either to change or to confirmation of the status quo.

How can one construct a theory that can accommodate such requirements? One possible starting point is the refutation—by the new pragmatist philosophy—of the metaphor of science as 'the mirror of the mind', where the mind itself was supposed to be a receptor of the 'true world' (Rorty 1980).

The ground for this kind of refutation had been prepared by the many variations of constructivism—from Schützian phenomenology, carried on by Berger and Luckmann (1966) and Holzner (1968) to Goodman's (1978) 'irrealist' claim that we are all world-makers. The realist ontology has turned into a belief, and a very practical one. Levine (1993) recalls a routine conversation with a 'true' scientist who invariably asked him at parties whether a deconstructionist (or a constructionist, for that matter) would die falling off a high tower. To which Levine supposedly (and routinely) responded that he would not know before seeing the event, but that he expected any deconstructionist of his acquaintance to steer safely away from the edges of high towers. It is practical to *believe* in the world of causes 'out there'; it works most of the time. This does not equal saying that there are ways of describing this world that represent it 'as it is': 'We need to make a distinction between the claim that the world is out there and the claim that truth is out there' (Rorty 1989: 4). As a consequence, the sophisticated notion of *episteme* (knowledge) becomes equivalent to the primitive *doxa* (opinion) (Rorty 1991*a*). What we know is what we believe to know. Researchers, like all other people, have opinions on all kinds of matters (indeed, the 'self' can be seen as a constantly reweaving web of beliefs) and test them in action; as a result, what works matters usually more than what is 'true' (besides, for whom is it true? for how long?). It is—sometimes—*the object of those opinions* and—always—*the conventional* (for given time and space) *way of expressing it that form differences between 'science' and 'everyday knowledge' or 'science' and 'literature'*.

Science, in this view, is a conversation of humankind, and its logic of enquiry is rhetorical (Oakeshott 1959/1991; McCloskey 1986). Much of this conversation takes place in written form, thus making it legitimate to apply various kinds of literary analysis to it—for instance, genre analysis.

IS MANAGEMENT AND ORGANIZATION THEORY A GENRE?

A genre is usually conceived as a system of action that became institutionalized and is recognizable by repetition; its meaning stems from its place within symbolic systems making up literature and culture, acquiring specificity by difference from other genres (Bruss 1976: 5). Is organization theory a genre in this sense?

Following Sandelands's third interpretation of the connection between theory and practice, I propose to treat theory production as a kind of practice.[6] This kind of practice produces insights that can serve as a source of inspiration and interesting associations to another practice. Consequently, disciplines such as business administration, management science, etc., should be eager to remain in close contact with management practice, with the purpose not of dictating the norms, but of reflecting and provoking. Thus, the art of writing (and of speaking—the persuasive skills in general) become extremely important, and their critical development a crucial task in its own right.

It is this understanding of organization science—as a practice, that is, as a

---

[6]   I hasten to add that these operations are not approved of by Lance Sandelands himself. It is important to differentiate between the author and the text. It is the latter that I engage here.

system of action that became institutionalized and recognizable—that makes the notion of organization theory analogous to that of a literary genre. After all, all organization researchers do is read (listen) and write (speak). So in that sense Astley and Zammuto (1992) were correct: organization researchers are involved in a linguistic practice. But there is more to it than 'just talking': it is important to point out that texts are actions (strictly speaking, material traces of such, but they both result from action and provoke further action), and actions are texts, in the sense that they must be legible to qualify as actions at all, and not, let us say, movements or behaviors.[7] 'Action' and 'text' are good metaphors of each other, but even more than that (Ricœur 1981: 197–221). Actions, especially institutionalized actions, produce texts; texts not only 'fix' other actions—their production and interpretation assume actions.

Actions, in order to be legible, must relate to some context accessible to those who attempt to make sense of them (Harré and Secord, 1972) and such a relation can be seen as a constraint. Just what such constraints and the ways of dealing with them are is well rendered in a description of a literary genre:

All reading (or writing) involves us in choice: we choose to pursue a style or a subject matter, to struggle with or against a design. We also choose, as passive as it all may seem, to take part in an interaction, and it is here that generic labels have their use. The genre does not tell us the style or the construction of a text as much as how we should expect to 'take' that style or mode of construction—what force it should have for us. And this force is derived from a kind of action that text is taken to be.   (Bruss 1976: 4)

The term 'choice' should not mislead the reader into assuming a rational choice: what Bruss calls 'a passive choice' can also be understood as following the 'logic of appropriateness', as March and Olsen (1989) call the usual logic of action that aims not at the choice of an optimal alternative but at an action that will be recognized and accepted by an audience residing within the same institutional set-up.[8] A student of mine described his methodological choices with the help of a garbage-can model: a given method results from a meeting between a certain type of advisers, doctoral students, accessible companies, and fashionable methods at the same time and place (Strannegård 1998).

In the sense of evoking expectations by using a label, organization theory is undoubtedly a genre; perhaps, in fact, more a genre than a discipline. A useful reflection could then focus on what are the constraints and possibilities of this genre, how does it develop historically, and what are its actual and potential connections to other genres.

Genre analysis is often used as a classificatory device (for the most famous example, see Northrop Frye, 1957/1990). Although a system of categories as such is relatively easy to construct and has a strong heuristic power, its application to concrete works is more problematic. After all, a genre is but a space within which one can position various works, and it would be their vicinity or

7   It should be clear by now, that in this notion of action no agency is implicated: actions are events to which intentions have been ascribed.

8   On the difference between the logic of action and the logic of decision, see Brunsson (1985).

distance to other works that would establish their genre. Genre analysis in literature places most works between genres; disagreement thus remains as to where the genre borders should run and whether it makes sense to draw them at all (Lejeune 1989). The best-known attempt at genre analysis within organization theory, Burrell and Morgan's (1979) classification of main paradigms, revealed its heuristic power in provoking massive protests and reclassifications. One can thus envisage an alternative to creating an interpretative space which will be able to contain and relate to each of many other approaches without ascribing strict positions to them. McCloskey (1986: p. xix) suggested, for instance, that literary criticism can offer economics a model for self-understanding: 'Literary criticism does not merely pass judgments of good or bad; in its more recent forms the question seems hardly to arise. Chiefly *it is concerned with making readers see how poets and novelists accomplish their results'* (emphasis added).

Such reflection, or self-reflection, makes a genre more distinct and more elaborated. The analysis of a genre is one of its main constitutive forces. Social scientists busy themselves constructing the institutions they describe. Describing what they do, organization researchers can increase the legitimacy of their own genre.

Not everybody is of that opinion. There are voices saying that problematizing what one does is not a good way to institutionalize it, that attracting attention to the process, inevitably exposing its messiness and lack of a priori criteria, is the last thing a discipline in need of legitimation wants (Pfeffer 1993). This might be true in the case of disciplines that are just beginning, which are vulnerable to any doubt, but different cycles in life require different legitimation tactics. The most established disciplines, such as philosophy, mathematics, or theoretical physics, like nothing more than a public soul-searching in order to renew and relegitimate themselves. This is helped by the fact that the very attempt to define a genre, as Lejeune (1989) pointed out, is paradoxical: it can only be done by exploring the gray zones and borderline cases. Genres blur as soon as you look at them at close range.

Neither paradoxicality nor the presence of conflict needs to debilitate a field; on the contrary, they enhance its controlling power. Institutions emerge and renew themselves 'by generating just the right kind of tension or even conflict, creative rather than destructive' (MacIntyre 1981/1990: 171). Delineating borders facilitates transgressions, stabilizing gives a basis for experimentation, routinizing permits improvisation. As language renews itself via paradox (Lyotard 1979/1987), so social practices renew themselves via tensions and contradictions. The approach suggested here can thus be seen as a loan from literary theory that will problematize organization theory, thus enabling it to reinvigorate itself.

Until now, I have argued for loans from literary theory in pragmatic terms: the dialogue between management theory and practice can thus be improved. But what legitimacy does such a move have? Does it not shake the position of scientific theory as distinct and separate from literature and journalism? In the two chapters that follow I attempt to build such a legitimacy base by showing that narratives abound in scientific theory. I begin by contrasting narrative and logico-scientific knowledge (Chapter 2), and then apply the distinction to exemplars of organization theory (Chapter 3).

A reader convinced by my reasoning may then proceed to successive chapters that illustrate possible modes of such rapprochement. Chapter 4 shows that such a vicinity is neither new nor unknown in the annals of social sciences. Chapter 5 applies the notion of plot to the activity of structuring field reports. Chapter 6 suggests taking detective stories, a highly plotted genre, as a model for organization studies. Chapter 7 returns to the concerns of managerial practice, and their place in management theory.

The Narrative in Social Sciences and Organization Studies

After years of following the lead of natural sciences, our fate has again joined with that of anthropology, sociology, social psychology, the political sciences, the theory of law, and other disciplines or subdisciplines that took a 'linguistic turn' in the 1970s and 1980s and that seem to be taking a 'literary turn' in the 1990s. The importance of language as the instrument of reality construction was recalled at the same time as Wittgenstein became fashionable again (Wittgenstein 1953). A thus encouraged stream of reflection led to self-reflection, considering the kind of knowledge social sciences produce and the kind used in practice, and in consequence opening the door to *narrative knowledge*.

A NARRATIVE KNOWLEDGE

The notion of narrative knowing, a paraphrase of narrative understanding, was coined by a psychologist, Jerome Bruner (1986)[1] and contrasted to the logico-scientific mode traditionally seen as the only legitimate mode of knowing in science (also called paradigmatic). The narrative mode of knowing consists in organizing one's experience around the intentionality of human action. The *plot* is the basic means by which specific events, otherwise represented as lists or chronicles, are put into one meaningful whole. 'The company suffered unprecedented losses' and 'the Managing Director was forced to resign' are two events that call for interpretation. 'As a result of the company's suffering unprecedented losses, the Managing Director was forced to resign' is a narrative. The difference lies in temporal ordering and thus in a suggested connection between the two (where some kind of causality is the most usual type of

---

[1] In parallel with other similar formulations. Lyotard (1979/1987), for instance, speaks about 'narrative' versus 'scientific' knowledge.

connection). The same set of events can be organized by more than one plot ('The Managing Director was forced to resign in spite of the fact that he offered to make good for the company's unprecedented losses'), where they consequently acquire a different meaning. Plots can differ both in form and in substance. However, within one cultural tradition, there is usually a well-known repertoire of plots constituting a given convention.

This narrative form of knowing, which might appear exotic in the context of organization theory, is, in fact, very close to the tradition of empirical research known as *case studies*. The popularity of such studies among practitioners and the resistance that academic research has shown towards them can be better understood if we notice that 'cases' are in fact very close to what are sometimes called 'folk theories'—that is, people's non-scientific explanations and interpretations of real-life events. But this disrespectful label is also arrogant. Narrative knowledge can be of use in a way that the logico-scientific form cannot. Narratives are most crucial in establishing connections between the exceptional and the ordinary. So-called 'folk psychology' thrives on the ordinary, on what is 'normal', usual, and expected, attributing to it legitimacy and authority. At the same time, however, it has at its disposal effective means for rendering the unexpected intelligible.

As stories explaining deviations are socially sensitive, a story form whose power does not reside in the difference between fact and fiction but in a *convincing interpretation* is convenient for the negotiation of meaning. One or many alternative narratives are always in the offing: 'Forced by the intrigues within the Board, the Managing Director resigned. The result was such a fall in morale of the personnel that the company suffered unprecedented losses.' Yet another story ('the Managing Director took with him all the subcontractors and as a result . . .') might offer a better, or more convincing explanation, without ever challenging the truth or the falsity of the elements. We have now four versions of the story about 'the Managing Director and the losses', all built around the same events. There is no other way to decide between them than to negotiate. And narratives, claims Bruner, are 'especially viable instruments for social negotiation'. This is why organizational stories are of such importance to researchers; in all their different versions, they capture organizational life in a way that no compilation of facts ever could.

The narrative mode of knowing is gaining a growing relevance for organization studies (Czarniawska 1997; 1998). This does not mean that it has to compete with the logico-scientific mode; the two can coexist in organization theory just as they do in organizational practice. But the ambition to produce narrative knowledge changes the task of the researcher: instead of reproaching the practice and telling the practitioners which way to go, our task would be to tell them a good story. In a good story, the events are its facts, and the point is its theory. A story without a point is meaningless; so are field reports that are not informed by theoretical insight. A story that just tells its point is not a story at all; it belongs to another world of thought, the logico-scientific one (see Chapter 4).

From the perspective adopted in the present discussion, narrative knowledge is an attractive candidate for bridging the gap between theory and practice. A narrative is able to produce generalizations and deep insights without claiming universal status (it may be that, in this world, general managers usually resign when troubles are brewing, but this is to be decided by a reader, not 'proven' by an author). A narrative is also able to transfer tacit knowledge without directly verbalizing it (a reader can 'imitate' it, as happens in learning by observation). Finally, it is possible to translate a narrative into a logico-scientific theory (although one would need many narratives) and into a plan of action (a 'local translation'). The reverse translation is also possible, but it requires that both logico-scientific theory and action plans must renounce their proper vocabularies and grammars to become narratives.

This double translation is not new or unknown. After all, says McCloskey (1986), 'sciences' such as economics always come up with nothing more, nothing less, than metaphors and stories. The difficulty lies in admitting this. Metaphors gained an easier acceptance because of their affinity to models. Stories have had a harsher lot (McCloskey 1990b).

By the criteria of scientific (paradigmatic) knowledge, the knowledge carried by narratives is not very impressive. Formal logic rarely guides the reasoning, the level of abstraction is low, and the causal links may be established in a wholly arbitrary way. As Lyotard (1979/1987) has pointed out, the legitimacy of scientific knowledge in its modern and Western meaning depends on its sharp differentiation from the common-sense, everyday knowledge of ordinary people—the narrative knowledge that tells of human projects and their consequences as they unfold over time. And yet it has been claimed that the narrative is the main mode of human knowledge (Bruner 1986; 1990) and the main mode of communication (Fisher 1984; 1987).

Reconciliation between scientific and narrative knowledge has now and again been attempted. In modern times, the examples of such attempts start with the work of Giambattista Vico (1744/1960), continue with the Realist novel (see Chapter 5), and the Chicago School of Sociology (see e.g. Cappetti 1995). How can they be justified?

Alasdair MacIntyre (1981/1990), a moral philosopher, claimed that social life is best conceived of as an enacted narrative. This is a thought resonant with that of a US philosopher, poet and literary theorist Kenneth Burke (1945/1969), who suggested a *dramatist* analysis of human conduct, which he based on the assumption that the rules of the drama reflect as much as influence and shape the actual social life. Thus he postulated a pervasive presence of a dramatist pentad that consists of Scene, Agent, Agency, Purpose, and Act (see Chapter 5).

This scheme for conceptualizing human action is indeed congruent with many an insight of famous social scientists. It is impossible to understand human conduct by ignoring its intentions, and it is impossible to understand human intentions by ignoring the settings in which they make sense, postulated Schütz (1973). Such settings may be institutions, sets of practices, or some other contexts created by humans and non-humans—contexts that have a history, that have been organized as narratives themselves. Particular deeds and whole histories of individual actors have to be situated in order to be intelligible. 'The Managing Director was forced to resign' is a meaningless sentence and if it is to acquire meaning it must be situated in the life history of this director or in the history of the profession or of the company. One problem of professional women these days might be not that they lack role models, but that they lack an appropriate repertoire of narratives that can help them to situate their own career narrative.

The advantages of building a connection between the theory of human action and the narrative has also been pointed out by Ricœur (1981), who suggested that meaningful action is to be considered as a text and text as an action. Meaningful action shares the constitutive features of the text: it becomes objectified by inscription, which frees it from its agents. It has relevance beyond its immediate context and it can be read like an 'open text'. The theory of interpretation can thus be extended to the field of social sciences (Ricœur 1981).

Will not social science lose more than it will gain if such extension was to take place? Polkinghorne (1987), following Ricœur's reasoning, pointed out that there is a special type of explanation that is possible only in a narrative. Only there can 'understanding' be reconciled with 'explanation' in an interpretation of the text. Hermeneutics and semiotics, which are but two sets of devices, can be combined in the same way as 'motives' are reconciled with 'causes' in an interpretation of human action, and justification is interwoven with causality in human beliefs (Rorty 1991a). This combination is looked down upon within science but is taken as obvious in the narrative: 'Tough competition made companies tighten their internal control system, which had often been used as a pretext to fire troublesome employees.' Within the logico-scientific mode of knowing, an explanation is achieved by recognizing an event as an instant of general law or as belonging to a certain category: 'Managing Directors, because of their symbolic status, are often first to go.' Within the narrative mode of knowing, an explanation consists in relating an event to human projects—'The Director's talents and commitment were of no importance to the scared Board.' 'Sensemaking' (more about it in Weick 1995) basically consists of attempts to integrate a new event into a plot, whereby it becomes understandable in relation to the context of what has happened. 'Thus, narratives *exhibit* an explanation instead of demonstrating it' (Polkinghorne 1987: 21).

While it is clear that the narrative offers an alternative mode of knowing, the relative advantage of using this mode may remain uncertain. Jerome Bruner (1990: 44) points out that the strength of the narrative lies in its indifference to extralinguistic reality. In narrative, it is the perceived *coherence* of the sequentiality (temporal order of events) rather than the truth or falsity of story elements that determines the plot, and thus the power of the narrative as a story. A story that says, 'The company suffered unprecedented losses, and then it started to snow'—that is, a story with an incomprehensible plot—will need some additional elements to make sense, even though the two events and their temporal connection may well be true and correct in themselves. In other words, there are no structural differences between fictional and factual narratives, and their respective attraction is not determined by their claim to be fact or fiction. Paul Veyne, a French historian, studied the notion of truth in history and said that 'A world cannot be inherently fictional; it can be fictional only according to whether one believes in it or not. The difference between fiction and reality is not objective and does not pertain to the thing itself: it resides in us, according to whether or not we subjectively see in it a fiction' (1988: 21). The interpretation of a narrative—both of its status (fact or fiction?) and of its point (scapegoating or not?)—is situationally negotiated or, rather, arrived at, since contingency plays as much a part in the process as aesthetics or politics. While the narrative may be indifferent to extralinguistic reality, it compensates for it with an extreme sensibility to the linguistic reality.

These characteristics of the narrative are noted by most of the analysts of the narrative, but are then often put aside with some embarrassment, to be triumphantly dragged out again by the advocates of the logico-scientific mode of knowing. What kind of knowledge is it that does not allow for recognizing whether or not a story is true or invented?

But Jerome Bruner claims that this peculiarity of narrative accounts for most of its power. People's non-scientific explanations and interpretations of life events are grounded in attempts to establish a connection between the exceptional and the ordinary. The ordinary, that which is 'normal', 'usual', and expected, acquires legitimacy and authority. The narrative, however, also has effective means at its disposal for rendering the unexpected intelligible. 'The function of the narrative is to find an intentional state that mitigates, or at least makes comprehensible, a deviation from a canonical cultural pattern' (Bruner 1990: 49–50).

This is all very well as long as it concerns everyday narratives. But can stories acquire a legitimate place in science? As I said before, the insight that scientific knowledge is grounded in metaphorical thinking has been more or less commonly accepted (thanks to writers such as Kuhn 1964/1996; McCloskey 1986; Morgan 1986). But, says McCloskey (1990a: 96), metaphors cannot live without stories: 'Stories criticize metaphors and metaphors criticize stories.' 'Scapegoat' is one metaphor that could be illustrated by the story above; but there are perhaps better stories for this metaphor and better metaphors for this story. Metaphors condense stories and stories examine metaphors.

Stories and metaphors cannot replace one another because they have different tasks to accomplish. A narrative is a mode of association, of putting different things together (and, and, and), whereas metaphor is a mode of substitution (or, or, or) (Latour 1988b). Alternatives to a narrative are lists and formal logic. An alternative to a metaphoric mode of substitution is, for instance, labeling—that is, giving proper names to objects and phenomena. There is a convention, however, that apportions different modes of association and substitution to different fields (science, literature) and different times (pre-modern, modern). Chapter 3 will be dedicated to the issues of space; let me now tackle the issues of time.

MODERN OR 'PRIMITIVE'?

Comparative studies of literate and non-literate societies (Goody 1986) show that, while narratives exist in both oral and literate cultures, there are three forms of text that became possible only because of the existence of the script: tables, lists, and recipes. The first two differ from the narrative in that they present items of information in a disjointed, abstracted way. In order to memorize a list or a table, a mnemonic device is required to make up for the lack of connections. The recipe assumes a chronological connection and thus seems to resemble a narrative, but it lacks the propelling force of a cause or an intention—the plot of the narrative. Clouds lead to rain and greed leads to crime; sifting the flour does not lead to breaking eggs. The recipe fulfills the learning function of the narrative in that it provides the learner with a vicarious experience—but in a way that is closer to that of tables or lists. One could say that recipes are lists, but of actions, not of objects.

Tables, lists, and recipes are undoubtedly the modern props of organizational knowledge. But if we agree with Latour (1993) that we have never become completely modern, then it can be interesting to take a look at non-modern modes of knowing that are still present in contemporary organizations.

In their eager desire to be as modern (and scientific) as possible, contemporary organizations tend to ignore the role of narrative in learning, at least in their programmatic attempts to influence organizational learning. Tables and lists (many 'models' and taxonomies are complicated lists) are given priority as teaching aids. Again, while they can fulfill certain functions which narratives cannot, the reverse applies even more. Almost certainly the greater part of organizational learning happens through the circulation of stories. Also, the extent to which the modern props of learning—and the technologies of writing that support them—are used in organizations varies. My own studies of city management revealed, for example, that in the Stockholm city office many important deals were made on the phone, whereas in Warsaw every agreement had to be confirmed in writing. Stockholm, however, was flooded with leaflets, brochures, and memos, whereas in Warsaw there were very few of these and important information was conveyed face-to-face only. Oral cultures are not necessarily ages away.

Studying collective memory in non-literate societies, Goody and Watt (1968: 30–1) pointed out that

The social function of memory—and forgetting—can thus be seen as the final stage of what may be called the homeostatic organization of the cultural tradition in non-literate society. The language is developed in intimate association with the experience of the community, and it is learned by the individual in face-to-face contact with the other members. What continues to be of social relevance is stored in the memory while the rest is usually forgotten . . .

But is this something exotic, never to be met in literate societies? To begin with, as Goody and Watt noted themselves, non-literate societies have various mnemonic techniques at their disposal. Secondly, their description of the non-literate community can be applied to any interpretive community in which written texts play a role secondary to that of oral or quasi-oral communication, facilitated by the modern media (telephone, Internet). It could be said of any contemporary company that 'what continues to be of social relevance is stored in the memory while the rest is usually forgotten'. As Goody and Watt observe, the oral tradition remains the primary mode of cultural orientation even in a literate culture, which is rather fortunate in the light of the unlimited variety and fragmentation of the written sources available. And the oral tradition depends on the narrative.

How does a collective memory work? An answer to this question requires a return to that other operation conceived as modern and scientific that, however, anthropology of knowledge reveals as ancient: categorization and classification (Durkheim and Mauss 1903/1963). Mary Douglas (1986), reviving the Durkheimian tradition, criticized two prominent notions of social theory, so crucial to organization theory: the assumption of the steady evolution of human consciousness and, consequently, of an irreparable breach between 'primitive' and 'modern' societies. Knowledge of the former, in face of this breach, would give no advantage for understanding the latter. Durkheim, she pointed out, shared this assumption but luckily failed to pursue it consistently. He introduced the notion of two forms of solidarity or grounds for collective action: classification—that is, belongingness to the same group (primitive societies)—and economy—that is, exchange (modern societies). Although he mourned the primitive solidarity as lost in modern societies, he nevertheless put much effort, together with Marcel Mauss, into understanding the classificatory work performed by institutions.

Now, when the supposed breach between 'primitive' and 'modern' societies has been definitively called in question (Lyotard 1979/1987; Latour 1993), the work of Durkheim and Mauss can be brought to bear on contemporary societies. While the turn the collective action takes may be mainly due to economic motives, it still acquires direction from shared classifications. And, although the work of classifying and negotiating classifications continues all the time in all kinds of interaction, it is facilitated and made possible by shared classifications of greater stability—the institutions. 'Institutions systematically direct individual memory and channel our perceptions into forms compatible with the relations they authorize. They fix processes that are essentially dynamic, they hide their influence, and they rouse our emotions to a standardized pitch on standardized issues' (Douglas 1986: 92). And later: 'The high triumph of institutional thinking is to make the institutions completely invisible' (p. 98). This restates what Lyotard said about scientific knowledge having been legitimized by a meta-narrative (of progress) and then disavowing the narrative knowledge of its legitimacy.

This effacement can be undone with no risk of a black hole of nihilism awaiting it from behind. That facts are produced (a 'fact' long known to anyone who bothered to check the etymology of the word) is no reason for despair, says Karin Knorr Cetina (1994: 8). Modern institutions including science run on fictions, as all institutions always did, and the task of the scholar is to study how these fictions are constructed and sustained. A narrative approach will reveal how institutional classifications are made, and will thus render the works of science more comprehensible. This statement of Knorr Cetina can be paraphrased by replacing 'the works of science' with 'management and organization'. Indeed, the narrative was present in organization studies even before its presence became legitimate.

NARRATIVE ON AND IN ORGANIZATIONS

Narrative enters organization studies in many forms. One, of which this text is an example, is a disciplinary reflection that resembles the literary critique. This was attempted first by John Van Maanen (1988). Although his 'tales of the field' were not focused on organization studies only, but on ethnographies in general, his work can be said to have legitimized the literary kind of reflection within the discipline. Sandelands and Drazin (1989), Sandelands (1990), and then Astley and Zammuto (1992) and Sköldberg (1994) began a debate on organization-theory language, audience, and the criteria of 'goodness', which still continues. Karen Golden-Biddle and Karen Locke (1993; 1997) analyzed textual strategies employed in organizational ethnographies, and the work that goes into the journal articles, while Ellen O'Connor (1996) did a close reading of the classics. The hope is that, thanks to those excursions into the narrative, organization studies will become more skilful in crafting their own narratives (for a similar view, see Hatch 1996).

There are, however, a great many ways in which narrative enters organization studies that study practices of the field. Fig. 2.1 is an attempt to map them, as it were, showing how they move from the field of managerial practice to that of academic practice. Chronologically, collecting stories was done earlier than studies of how stories are being made. It started as early as with the works of Clark (1972) and Mitroff and Kilman (1975). Organizational stories actually became a legitimate topic of organization studies in the 1980s, as exemplified in the works of Joanne Martin and her collaborators (e.g. Martin 1982; Martin *et al.* 1983).

Such stories from the field were at first treated as material to be interpreted by field researchers. They have, however, increasingly been retold in a slightly stylized way in the belief that they can teach young students the practices of the field much more successfully than texts written in a scientific mode. In this

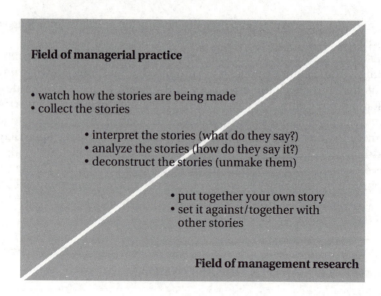

Fig. 2.1. The possible uses of the narrative approach in field research

context at least two examples, both focusing on Anglo-Saxon organizations, are worth mentioning: Frost, Mitchell, and Nord (1978 and subsequent editions), and Sims, Gabriel, and Fineman (1993).

In the 1990s attention has been attracted to the ways stories are made. Boland and Tankasi (1995) criticized well-known studies from the 1980s for their view of organizational narratives as artefacts forever petrified in organizational reality, 'out there' waiting to be 'collected'. Thus researchers such as Boje (1991), Boland himself (1989; 1994), Forester (1992), Gabriel (1995), Yanow (1996), and Barry and Elmes (1997) began to accentuate the process of storytelling as the never-ending construction of meaning in organizations.

Weick (1995) made this the focus of his most recent book. While much of organizational life is actually spent on reading the stories already made, and interpreting them within a set of already existing rules (routines), there also exists sensemaking or the activity of attributing meaning to previously meaningless cues. Weick explored seven properties of organizational sensemaking: 'identity, retrospect, enactment, social contact, ongoing events, cues, and plausibility' (1995: 3). After discussing plausibility (which in organizational practice is much more important than accuracy—the fetish of perception studies), Weick thus summarized the most important aspects of sensemaking:

If accuracy is nice but not necessary in sensemaking, than what is necessary? The answer is, something that preserves plausibility and coherence, something that is reasonable and memorable, something that embodies past experience and expectations, something which resonates with other people, something that can be constructed retrospectively but also can be used prospectively, something that captures both feeling and thought, something that allows for embellishment to fit current oddities, something that is fun to contrast. In short, what is necessary in sensemaking is a good story.   (1995: 60–1)

This, in Weick's opinion, is what is most needed 'in an equivocal, postmodern world, infused with the politics of interpretation and conflicting interests' (1995: 61). This is consistent with the postulate of requisite variety, known from his earlier work, suggesting that complex objects must be met by complex models (Weick 1979). Although stories simplify the world, and are therefore useful as guides for action, they simplify it less than the kind of formal models that used to be revered as genuine science.

Organizational narratives, as the main mode of knowing and communicating in organizations, must become an important focus for organization researchers. Their construction and reproduction need to be documented and their contents interpreted. Narrative forms of reporting will enrich organization studies themselves, complementing, illustrating, and scrutinizing logico-scientific forms of reporting. By relinquishing some aspirations to power through the claim of factuality and one-to-one correspondence of theory and the world, organization studies can open their texts for negotiations and thus enter in a dialogical relationship with organizational practice.

THE FIELD AS READ

Such an approach would also permit us to widen the accessible repertoire of actions to be taken 'in between the two worlds': interpreting, analyzing, and deconstructing the stories from the field.[2] There exists a well-established interpretivist tradition, described first by Burrell and Morgan (1979), solidified by Putnam and Pacanowsky (1983), and cultivated by studies in the symbolist tradition (Pondy et al. 1983; Frost et al. 1985; Gagliardi 1990; Turner 1990). Text analysis and deconstruction begin to appear more and more often (for the early examples see Martin 1990 and Calás and Smircich 1991). Let me make a short inventory of things to be done to the stories collected in the field.

Such stories come in many guises: some are written in numbers, some in words; some are written by the researcher (e.g. interview records and field notes) and some by other people (e.g. documents and press clippings). This does not matter all that much; the task is to interpret them and to come up with a new text that will bear this interpretation.

There is a host of interesting options for those who need to read the texts from the field. There exist excellent instructions on how to proceed (see e.g. Silverman and Torode 1980 on interruption; Martin 1990 on deconstruction; Riessman 1993 on narrative analysis; Silverman 1993 on conversation analysis;

---

[2]   This section and the one that follows rely closely on Czarniawska (1998).

Feldman 1995 on ethnomethodology, semiotic analysis, dramaturgical analysis, and deconstruction).

A field-research report is, therefore, a compilation of texts authored by practitioners, theoreticians, and the author her- or himself. The analogy that comes to mind is that of a literary *collage* (after all, our computer says 'paste'), although, in deference to Walter Benjamin, it is often called a literary *montage* (see e.g. Cappetti 1995; Pred 1995). A collage also makes visible that particular mixture of reproduction and production that every reading and writing necessarily entails.

There are two aspects that need to be brought to the fore in relation to the collage analogy. I maintain that, while field reports always were collages, work and skill were put into softening the edges, erasing the different authorships, achieving the illusion of one voice telling one story. Calling the research report a collage is an encouragement to make it clearly polyphonic, where the authorship of different pieces is distinctly attributed.

This does not mean that the role of the reader/writer should be effaced. Collage is the work of an author, and the pieces used acquire a new meaning by being recontextualized. Polyphony is actually nothing other than a *variegated speech*, as Bakhtin/Medvedev (1928/1985)[3] said, a writer's trick that enriches the text but also, more importantly, reminds readers that the world is full of different voices, differing vocabularies, and disparate dialects, that there cannot be one story of the world. I shall discuss these issues at length in the last chapter.

But even gluing disparate pieces together amounts to an act of reading. It is, therefore, not out of place to recall the hermeneutic triad as a way of representing interpretive procedures of which many variations exist. I shall quote one by Hernadi (1987), who classifies interpretation into three stages: explication, explanation, and exploration. *Explication* is reproductive translation, where the interpreter chooses to stand *under* the text, in Frye's (1973) term, aiming at understanding it. The next stage, *explanation*, is an employment of an inferential detection to analyze it, where the reader stands *over* the text. This can be done in many ways depending on the preference of the reader. The conventional scientific analysis sees this stage as an explanation by reference to 'reality', whereas literary theory explains by reference to other texts. The former looks for traces of the world in the analyzed text (what is sometimes called 'a seepage from reality'); the latter looks for traces of other texts.

Social scientists have a professional duty to proceed to the third stage, that of *exploration*, where readers stand *in for* the author, thus constructing a new text although with an original one as a starting point. This might mean constructing a text from scratch (in opposition to the one already existing), a reconstruction, or a deconstruction of the one that exists.

Returning to the short narrative used in this book, the interpretation might go through all three stages as follows: 'This is a story of a Managing Director

---

[3]   The precise authorship of this work (and some others by Bakhtin) is uncertain.

who was fired in a time of economic crisis. She served as the symbol of tight-
ened control exerted by the Board of Directors. In her place, I would have gone
to the press and revealed the futility of such symbolic gestures.'

Such readings can be many and varied, but they can also happen at another
level. Imagine a reader who also goes through the three stages, but in the
following way: 'The original text is very short on detail, thus creating an ambiguity that permits many interpretations. This is typical for texts where the
authors expect the readers to project their own experience into the text. Such
a textual strategy might misfire, however, as the author is known to be a feminist and therefore her interpretation will be treated with suspicion.'

The first reading is close to the text, and represents an attitude that Eco
(1992) calls that of a *naïve (semantic)* reader. Such readers assume that the text
carries a message, and try to render this message either by direct quote, repetition, or retelling it; they look at the seepage from reality (is it true? how could
it have happened?) and identify with the author or the character in the stage of
exploration. *A semiotic (critical) reader* looks in the first place for a seepage
from other texts:

The former uses the work as semantic machinery and is the victim of the strategies of
the author who would lead him a little by little along the series of provisions of expectations. The latter evaluates the work as an aesthetic product and enjoys the strategies
implemented in order to produce a Model Reader of the first level [i.e. a semantic
reader]   (Eco, 1990: 92)

An aspiring semiotic reader often asks for help (semantic readers usually have
confidence in their 'natural' attitude). What should one look for? What do the
clues look like? How does one establish connections between one text and all
the others? Such questions are frequent, and there are some attempts to
answer them by turning to the formalized analytical techniques. But there are
no interpretation rules. The *Nudist* program creates only another text that
must be interpreted in its turn. As Ricœur (1981: 211) said, 'there are no rules for
making good guesses. But there are methods for validating guesses.' The operation of abduction as described by Peirce and practiced by Sherlock Holmes
(Eco and Sebeok 1983) is central in reading texts. Both semantic and semiotic
readings of the story of a Managing Director who was forced to resign entail
hypotheses: 'there are many such cases in organizations', and 'the author
wanted to push the readers into a projection mode'. In the first case, the readers must check the statistics; in the second, they must read the research paper
from which the text was excerpted. As it is easy to see, both checks require
contact with other texts, although the traditional methodology insists on calling the first check the 'reality check'.

The scrutiny of the activity of reading as presented above makes it clear that
reading and writing are inseparable. To read is always to write, even if sometimes without the material traces. To write is always to read, both in retrospec-
tion and in anticipation. It should thus come as no surprise that many
comments concerning the reading of a text of the field concern equally writing

a text from the field, and therefore most comments on writing concern, in fact, an anticipated reading.

THE FIELD AS WRITTEN

There exists organizational research that is written in a story-like fashion ('tales from the field', to paraphrase the expression in Van Maanen 1988). Goodall's *Casing a Promised Land: The Autobiography of an Organizational Detective as Cultural Ethnographer* (1994) is one of the most conscious attempts to write in this way, but—and this is my point—all of us who studied management as a practice engaged in story writing in one or another way. My plea is thus not very radical: to recognize officially that which is a common practice, and to cultivate it instead of apologizing for it.

The question thus arises, will the use of a narrative help us to write 'better' texts? If so, which texts are 'good'? An author tries to anticipate the readers' reaction in part by projecting the past criteria of the 'goodness' of a scientific text onto the future. I say 'in part' because all innovative writing hopes to establish new criteria by defying earlier ones. To be followed or to be broken, evaluation criteria seem to be helpful to a writer. A constructionist view, however, clearly reveals the impossibility of establishing such criteria a priori. There exists only a pattern of conventional readers' responses (known only retrospectively) and a bunch of institutionalized norms for writing that in practice might be observed or broken.

One traditional set of such norms refers to validity, the correspondence between the text and the world, and to reliability, the guarantee of repeated results with the use of the same method. These are supposedly ostensive traits: they characterize (or not) a text as it is, and therefore can be demonstrated.

Validity as a correspondence criterion has attracted most criticism from contemporary knowledge theorists. Whether we claim to speak of a reality or a fantasy, the value of our utterances cannot be established by comparing them to their object, but only by comparing them to other utterances, as Goffman (1981) noted, systematically comparing various forms of talk. As the new pragmatists put it, the correspondence theory of truth is untenable because the only thing with which we can compare statements are other statements (Rorty 1980). Words cannot be compared to worlds. A look into actual validation practices reveals that, in fact, they always consist in checking texts against other texts. Thus when Ricœur (1981) spoke of 'validation of guesses', he hastened to add that by this he did not mean the application of the logic of empirical verification: 'To show that an interpretation is more probable in the light of what is known is something other than showing that a conclusion is true. . . . Validation is an argumentative discipline comparable to the juridical procedures of legal interpretation' (p. 212).

It could be argued that, by the same token, an observation shows that there exists reliability understood as replication. From the perspective held here, however, it could be claimed that 'results' are repeated not because the correct method has repeatedly been applied to the same object of study, but because institutionalized research practices tend to produce similar results. One can go even further and claim that results are as much part of practice as are methods. An excellent illustration of this phenomenon is the recent debate within AIDS research, which shows that studies that do not arrive at what is seen as the legitimate conclusion are not funded (Horton 1996). It is perhaps more accurate to speak of 'conformity' rather than reliability; it is not the results that are reliable, but the researchers who are conforming to dominant rules.

Dissatisfaction with positivist criteria for 'good scientific texts' and a wish for alternative guidelines for their writers led to a search for a new set of criteria— within the interpretive tradition. Thus Guba (1981) spoke of 'trustworthiness' of naturalist studies (composed of truth value, applicability, consistency, and neutrality); Fisher (1987) spoke of 'narrative probability' (coherence) and 'narrative fidelity' (truth value), constituting 'narrative rationality'; while Golden-Biddle and Locke (1993) suggested authenticity, plausibility, and criticality as the ways in which ethnographic texts convince their audiences. Unfortunately, like the positivist criteria they criticize, these are again *ostensive* criteria of a text's success—that is, the attributes of a text that can be demonstrated and therefore applied a priori to determine a text's success.

Reader-response theory has counteracted such objectivist reading theories (Iser 1978), but, in turn, it tries to subjectivize the act of reading and therefore neglects the institutional effect. There is a limited repertoire of texts and responses at any given time and place, there are more legitimate and less legitimate responses, and there is fashion as a selection mechanism. The pragmatist theory of reading to which I adhere, best known in the rendition of Stanley Fish but here represented by Rorty (1992*b*), gives preference to *performative* criteria. These are not rules that, when observed by a writer, will guarantee the positive reception of his or her work, but descriptions that summarize the typical justifications given when a positive reception occurs. Such descriptions concern not the text but the responses of the readers as reported in the legitimate vocabulary of the day.

A contemporary organization-theory writer who desires success might thus do well choosing postmodernism as his or her mantle, but texts written in the peak of fashion might become classical or obsolete, and no properties of the text can determine what is going to be their fate. Friedrich Nietzsche was considered mad in his time, whereas Franz Anton Mesmer is now best remembered not for his thought or his therapy but for having been a success in his time.

The aspiring author cannot count on readers to tell what they are going to like next, but might try to collect accounts justifying their past judgements, and hope that they will hold for awhile. There are two types of justifications commonly given: the pragmatic and the aesthetic. It is even possible to claim that the latter is included in the former and vice versa, if treated broadly enough. Something 'works' because it touches me, because it is beautiful, because it is a powerful metaphor, but one can also hear engineers (and not only them) say of machines, 'look how beautifully it works!' Rorty (1992*b*) says that, although 'usefulness' is decided according to a purpose at hand, best readings are not those that serve such a purpose but that have changed it. This he calls an *edifying* discourse or a discourse that has the power 'to take us out of our old selves by the power of strangeness, to aid us in becoming new beings' (Rorty 1980: 360). Books like Silverman's *The Theory of Organizations* (1971), Weick's *The Social Psychology of Organizing* (1979), or Morgan's *Images of Organization* (1986) took us out of positivist methodology, out of open systems perspective, and out of essentialist conceptualization.

One could question the 'we' of the last paragraph, claiming that this last kind of reaction is personal (many organization researchers are still using the open-systems perspective) and therefore contingent on individual readers and their 'purpose at hand'. This is a correct observation, but it is equally correct to note that the purposes at hand and the ways of satisfying them tend to be limited in a given time and place. Objectivity, that high praise when addressed to scientific texts, can be seen as no more and no less than conformity to the norms of justification common in a relevant community (Rorty 1980: 36); a difficult achievement and *therefore* praiseworthy.

Judgements on what is objective and what is edifying are rarely unanimous (there is a variety of opinions in each community) and they change over time. Therefore one can at best speak of a kind of writing or rather kinds of writing that are considered legitimate, and that are read at a given time and place. The debate on what is good and bad writing can thus be usefully replaced or at least aided by a discussion of genres—that is, institutionalized forms of writing. Achieving an inventory and a description of genres helps not only to estimate chances of success, but also to understand deviations. Every avant-garde, every vibrant fringe, every edifying discourse feeds on the mainstream, on normal science, on systematizing discourse. By the same token, the 'canonical tradition' (MacIntyre 1988) depends on deviations for its survival, and also owes its eventual demise to them.

As long as a tradition can incorporate innovations, it is vitalized by them; the moment it cannot, it dies. This paradoxical relationship between the mainstream and the margin is well known but rarely openly recognized, as it threatens the grounds of legitimacy of both the mainstream and the margin. The legitimate vision of the relationships between the two is an agonistic relationship; as in a traditional science, the best man (yes) wins.

This reasoning can be applied to itself: it is possible to imagine a non-agonistic science, and an explicit awareness of the mutual dependence between the avant-garde and the retro-garde. Such views, although marginal at present, might repay in reflection and sophistication what they cost in legitimacy.

Let me then move to the actual genre analysis. I will start with various texts in organization theory, to show that they are employing textual strategies traditionally attributed to literature and therefore justify the further excursion into literary theory and practice.

A Four-Times-Told Tale: Combining Narrative and Scientific Knowledge in Organization Studies

Scholarship is customarily set apart from the everyday wisdom of ordinary people. Science should keep to facts and logic, leaving metaphors and stories to literature, this being a sediment of pre-modern times and oral societies. And yet, as, for example, McCloskey (1990a) pointed out, contrary to this received wisdom, the sciences can be said to be using a whole tetrad of rhetorical figures: stories, metaphors, facts, and formal logic. *Belles lettres* or 'folk theories' mainly use stories and metaphors, quite often fact, and sometimes even formal logic. Experimental writers and artists, such as Borges, Cortazar, Escher, and others with an inclination for linguistic and visual paradoxes, did play with logic.

On the other hand, social scientists seldom use formal logic—in the sense of the particular mode of reasoning, because all of them use logic in the sense of syntactic rules. What I want to emphasize is that 'science' is not separated from 'literature' by an abyss; over and above the publishers' classification, a work is also attributed to a certain genre according to the frequency with which it uses certain rhetorical devices. Umberto Eco, who is a legitimate citizen in both worlds, put it as follows:

I understand that, according to a current opinion, I have written some texts that can be labeled as scientific (or academic or theoretical), and some others which can be defined as creative. But I do not believe in such a straightforward distinction. I believe that Aristotle was as creative as Sophocles, and Kant as creative as Goethe. There is not some mysterious ontological difference between these two ways of writing . . . The differences stand, first of all, in the propositional attitude of the writer, even though their propositional [attitude] is usually made evident by textual devices . . .   (1992: 140)

We recognize a scientific text not because of its intrinsic scientific qualities, but because the author claims it is scientific (and this claim can be contested) and because he or she uses textual devices that are conventionally considered scientific (and this convention is contested all the time).

Several traditions within organization studies support this suggestion: for instance, case studies and a variety of interpretive approaches. Some collective reflection is needed to consolidate such efforts. This chapter represents an endeavor in this direction. The aim is to illustrate common ways of joining paradigmatic (model-like) and syntagmatic (story-like) elements in organization theory texts: a paradigmatic discussion illustrated by syntagmatic examples; a paradigmatic analysis retold syntagmatically; a syntagmatic story punctuated by paradigmatic points; a syntagmatic tale with a hidden paradigm.

The initial difficulty seems to lie in the unclear generic situation of the social sciences *vis-à-vis* natural science and literature (Lepenies 1988). Are social-science texts telling stories or reporting science? Following Latour (1992*a*), one can try to distinguish between these two kinds of text by saying that the former evolve along the *syntagmatic* dimension, grounded in association, and the latter along the *paradigmatic* dimension, based on substitution. A narrative thus adds various events one after another over time, while a scientific model substitutes a group of particulars by a more abstract concept that is intended to cover them all. Generalization, and consequently prediction, operate differently in the two modes. Syntagmatic construction uses metonymy;[1] it operates on the sense of part and whole (how things hang together). Paradigmatic construction, on the other hand, uses metaphor; it operates on the sense of like and unlike (similarity, analogy). Turning to the social-scientific texts, one cannot help noticing that both constructions appear: there are elements of the syntagmatic and the paradigmatic, of metonymy and metaphor, of narrative and logo-science. Fig. 3.1 (which may look trivial but in fact summarizes a whole book of mine (Czarniawska-Joerges 1989), illustrates such a typical mixture. By rearranging McCloskey's (1990*a*) tetrad somewhat (see fig. 3.2), Latour's insight can be incorporated into it. The horizontal dimension will then represent the syntagm: logic and stories as two modes of association, of establishing a connection—of connecting in actual time and space or, hypothetically or counterfactually, of connecting in possible worlds. Facts and metaphors denote two kinds of substitution—namely, the linguistic operations known as 'representation' and 'analogy'.[2] They constitute a dimension extended between the two modes of name-giving: 'facts' are names or assertions about which we tend to agree easily ('this is the recently acquired computer'), while metaphors indicate a stage of enquiry rather than consensus ('is this a cost or an investment?'). The extremes would be proper names and metaphors proper (with similes and analogies in between).

In fig. 3.2 'science' is no longer distinct from 'literature'. As I said before, a work is ascribed to a certain genre according to the frequency with which it uses certain rhetorical devices. McCloskey's tetrad now denotes a space within

---

[1]   Although not in a Burkean sense (Burke 1945/1969).

[2]   Although metaphor goes beyond analogy. Analogy assumes continuity, metaphor assumes rupture.

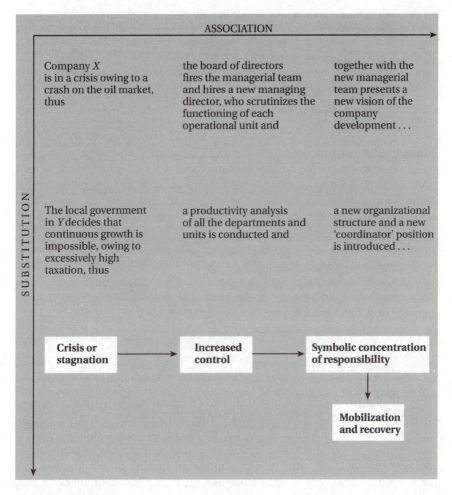

Fig. 3.1. Association and substitution (syntagmatic and paradigmatic dimensions) in organization studies

which one could position various works, and it would be their proximity to other similar works that would establish their genre. For example, metaphors (or models) seem to be more frequent in economics than stories, which are very frequent, on the other hand, in the subgenre known as economic history (McCloskey 1990*a,b*). Geertz (1973; 1988) stressed the obvious importance of stories in anthropology but he also pointed out that there are more metaphors than one would assume. A historical elucidation of the ties between stories and metaphors in sociology can be found in Lepenies (1988)—ties cultivated by phenomenologically inclined sociologists in, for example, R. H. Brown (1977; 1980) and, more recently, by the sociologists of science and technology in Mulkay (1985), Latour (1988*b*, 1992*b*), and Traweek (1992).

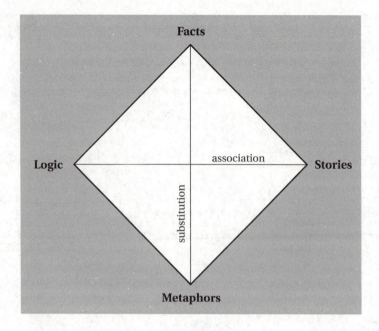

Fig. 3.2. Syntagm and paradigm as delimiting a generic space in which both literature and science live

In this chapter I will look at well-known organization studies, showing different ways (and degrees) in which they incorporate narrative in their production. The first example (James D. Thompson 1967) follows what is considered to be an ideal of scientific reasoning, attempting to form logical propositions, which in turn give metaphorical quality to the entities thus characterized. The next work (Brunsson 1989) constructs a metaphorical model, which is then retold in the form of stories. The third (Knorr Cetina 1981) collects stories from the field, and builds a theoretical model to interpret them. The fourth (Smircich 1985) invents a story that includes the metaphors it illustrates.

LOGIC—METAPHORS

James D. Thompson, *Organizations in Action: Social Science Bases of Administrative Theory* (New York: McGraw-Hill, 1967)

Although no official contest was ever held, Thompson's book is considered at least unofficially to be a model of rhetorical elegance in organization theory. Short and concise, it aims at covering all relevant issues and formulating the proper science of organizations according to scientific ideals—that is, as a set of formal (at least apparently formal) propositions.

My experience of various institutional settings in which organization theory is taught as a subject in Sweden evoked a puzzling observation. It seems that Thompson is rarely used as a course book in its home field—that is, in the departments of business administration (and then only in a course on 'classics')—but it is widely used in organization-theory courses taught in neighboring disciplines: education, psychology, sociology, political sciences. Part of the explanation lies, no doubt, in the specific way management is taught in Sweden: whereas the undergraduate courses mainly use textbooks in Swedish of a summarizing and popularizing character, the graduate courses take up the most recent research work or, indeed, 'the classics'.

But another complementary interpretation of this phenomenon takes us back to Thompson's text. Setting out to be exhaustive, to combine the incompatible (the rational system versus natural open systems approaches), embracing an impressive range of schools and sources (where Parsons and Goffman sit side by side), this is a striking example of how an accumulative knowledge achieves the closure of an intellectual field that, if taken seriously, could put an end to the discipline. If Thompson were to be taken literally, there would be no need for organization theory after him. And this is due in no small measure to the rhetorical style he adopts.

Here follow two excerpts from Thompson's book.

Proposition 4.1
Organizations under norms of rationality seek to place their boundaries around those activities which if left to the task environment would be crucial contingencies.

The implication of this proposition is that we should expect to find organizations including within their domains activities or competencies which, on a technological basis, could be performed by the task environment without damage to the major mission *of the organization. For the hotel, for example, provision of rooms and meals would be the major mission, and the operation of a laundry would be excluded; yet we find hotels operating laundries. On the other hand, provision of rooms and meals would not be within the major mission of the hospital, although hospitals commonly include these activities within their domains.*

The incorporation of subsidiary competencies along with major missions is commonplace in organizations of all types and is not a major discovery. But our proposition is not an announcement of the fact; rather it attempts to indicate the direction in which domains are expanding. (Thompson 1967: 39–40)

Proposition 6.1
Under norms of rationality, organizations facing heterogeneous task environments seek to identify homogenous segments and establish structural units to deal with each.

This proposition is perhaps most dramatically illustrated by the organization which crosses national boundaries where environmental variations may be stark. Under these conditions, organizations tend to establish semiautonomous divisions based on a region. Those organizations which dabble in foreign operations may simply have a foreign or non-domestic division; but when they become more deeply involved, they usually establish national or at least bloc entities . . .

We need not cross cultural boundaries to see this proposition in action. Public school systems divide themselves into elementary and secondary schools, and only in rare cases are these ungraded internally. General hospitals establish separate units for obstetrics, contagious diseases, and surgical and outpatient services; mental hospitals often establish separate units for various types of disorders or severity of problems. Universities create undergraduate and graduate divisions. Public-assistance agencies may be divided into different units for dispensing unemployment compensation benefits, and aid to dependent children or the blind.   (Thompson 1967: 70–1)

What does Thompson say? In translating his organizationalese into English, I follow McCloskey's (1986) example, although I am aware that this innocent 'translation' already heralds the readings I intend to make next. Briefly, Thompson says that organizations incorporate those activities that may be crucial to them in order to avoid dependency on their environment, and that they create internal units that correspond to unified (similar) portions of their environment.

This is stated in the form of theorems—that is, ideas 'accepted or proposed as a demonstrable truth often as a part of a general theory' (*Webster's New Collegiate Dictionary* 1981: 1200). Before turning to demonstrations, let us stay awhile with the propositions themselves. Their formulation follows the rules of logic, but they concern not 'facts' but tropes, of which the two most important are 'organization' and 'environment'.

'Organization' is clearly a synecdoche: that which is organized becomes an entity named after its attribute. The use of organizations in the plural, indicating an entity, and an entity that became the main subject of organization theory, appeared as late as the 1960s, with the advent of systems theory in the social sciences (Waldo 1961); in fact, Thompson still speaks of 'administration theory' (administration being the synonym of management, connected by usage with public authority rather than private enterprise). Even more interesting is 'environment': this central concept in organization theory is residual in character, meaning simply 'that which surrounds organizations'. As Meyer (1996) put it succinctly, the environment is the Other to the Actor, as the environment of a modern organization consists of other organizations (see also Perrow 1991).

Thus Thompson's propositions suggest logical connections between tropes; let us see how this is demonstrated. According to the rules of the (scientific) game, the demonstration cannot happen within the language (as one might expect in this context), but rather by reference to reality.

Thompson's demonstrations do not involve concrete facts: we learn nothing about an experiment conducted at laboratory *X* on date *Y*. The illustrations are formulated in a way that resembles and repeats propositions, but the abstract tropes are replaced by generic terms such as 'organizations which cross national boundaries', 'general hospitals', 'hotels'. The verbs remain in the simple present ('organizations tend to', 'organizations seek to identify').

An autobiographical anecdote might be helpful in solving this mystery: when studying for my comprehensive exams in economics (my doctoral dissertation required a transfer from social psychology to economics), I was struck by the peculiar style of the economic texts and asked my adviser[3] whether the constant use of the simple present meant that enterprises *are* actually doing these things, *have done* them, or *should be doing* them? 'None of these,' said my adviser. 'They are doing so in a mental model into which they have been designed—thus it is a tense which indicates their "unreal" state, as it were.'

But is this what Thompson intended? He himself said that 'our [*sic*] proposition is not announcement of the fact: rather it attempts to indicate the direction . . . '. By that, as the previous sentence indicates, he did not mean that this was a hypothetical move in a hypothetical model; he suggested that the proposition contained more than a mere fact (by now trite); it contained a prediction. Thompson used *prolepsis*: 'the representation or assumption of a future fact or development as if presently existing or accomplished' (*Webster's New Collegiate Dictionary* 1981: 913).

One could thus claim that Thompson's 'scientism' is but a stylization: the entities in question are in fact tropes, and could be connected only with one another; the postulated connections are achieved by the use of yet another rhetorical figure. It would be wrong, however, to conclude from this that Thompson failed to achieve the scientific status he aspired to; this is, in fact, the way scientific texts tend to look in the social sciences. Few of them even try to achieve such a strict stylization, and allow the stories to creep directly into their texts.

METAPHORS—STORIES

Nils Brunsson, *The Organization of Hypocrisy: Talk, Decision and Actions in Organizations* (Chichester: Wiley, 1989)

The choice of Brunsson's book might be objected to, in relation to its predecessor here: does it deserve to be called a 'classic', as Thompson's work undoubtedly does? It may, of course, be that the time of the 'classics' is irretrievably over, and in any case it is difficult to guess which contemporary works—if any—will become classics. Suffice it to say that Brunsson's book was reviewed seventeen times in the four years after its publication (Social Science Citation Index 1993), apart from reviews in the popular press: there were even reviews in the French popular press, which is not usually receptive to Anglo-Saxon publications.

Brunsson shared with Thompson an interest in taking up the rationalist and the institutionalist approaches to organizations. Instead of integrating them, however ('under the norms of rationality'), he expanded the ideas of Thurman Arnold (1935), suggesting that the two coexist in a functional hypocrisy, and that some effort is expended on keeping them apart ('decoupling'). The

---

[3]   Prof. Janusz Beksiak of the Warsaw School of Economics.

public-administration organizations (state and municipal), which interested him, have a dual basis for their legitimacy: politics and action. 'It is expected that they should reflect a variety of values and that they should run reasonably efficient operations' (Brunsson 1989: 33).

The basic method for handling these conflicting demands is to separate and isolate politics and action, to 'decouple' them . . .

. . . *politics and action can be separated organizationally: some units can respond to political demands and are organized in such a way as to resemble the ideal political type, while other units can respond to demands for action and are organized in a way that closely resembles the ideal type of the action organizations. Municipalities and the state typically possess a number of variously politicized suborganizations. As we have seen, parliaments and social councils are strongly political units which produce talk and decision in public arenas. Governments and committees hold closed meetings and are more action-oriented.*

The organization can also be divided into one part run by politicians and one part run by the administration. Politicians are recruited according to the principle of conflict, while administrative officials are recruited according to the principle of unity. In other organizations boards can be politically composed, while management and production departments are based on the idea of unity. In this way the organization as a whole can respond to demands for both politics and action—so long as the two units really are isolated from one another. . . .

The political and administrative dichotomy becomes more problematic if the organization tries to link the political and administrative suborganizations together, i.e. if the decisions of the political unit are to be made consistent with the actions of the action unit, or vice versa. This problem arises when it is claimed that the decisions of the leadership should steer administrative action—which is not an unusual idea. (Brunsson 1989: 37)

Thompson in his proposition 6.1, and Brunsson above, seem to be speaking on the same theme: one of the ways 'organizations' 'adapt' to their 'environments'. The main tropes are still in place, although Brunsson enriches them with two more ('politics' and 'action'[4]). The picture has become more complex: the environment cannot be entirely divided into 'homogeneous segments'; in some segments (political ones) it seems that heterogeneity is the characteristic feature. Also, readers learn not only how organizations act, but what use organizational actors make of it. Thompson kept a behaviorist distance from 'organizations': this is how they act, 'under the norms of rationality'. Brunsson took the resulting structure not as an answer, but as a question, and went on to investigate the processes that created such a structure.

In doing so he started with 'propositions' not altogether unlike Thompson's, which claim general connections but without the stylization of formal logic. His general statements are not so much propositions as summaries, to be explicated by examples of concrete organizations in concrete situations. Contrary to the suggestion contained in the sentence 'As we have seen . . .', his metaphors

---

[4]   Both of them naturally employ a whole plethora of other tropes, subordinate or complementary to the main ones.

do not emerge from his stories (at least in the text; it is not my ambition to detect the actual intellectual operations performed by the authors). The present reader must trust me in that 'we' have not seen anything yet; the sentence alludes to earlier abstract formulations. The examples come later to illustrate general statements. The quotation below describes a crisis in Runtown, a small municipality in southern Sweden, where the externally induced crisis led to a striving for unity (tighter coupling), which only deepened the crisis.

Between 1973 and 1976 external crises were succeeded by internal troubles—which did not mean, however, that the external problems had gone away. . . . There were certain signs that attitudes were changing. . . . Everyone wanted to see a new kind of behaviour and more action.

At the beginning of the period there were even a few results. . . . The new administrators energetically pursued the question of long-range economic planning and eventually persuaded the politicians to agree to a document specifying municipal goals. This, they felt, would put their own operations on a firmer basis, since the politicians would have to become a little less volatile. The politicians had no difficulty in agreeing to these goals, which were expressed in very general terms and seemed unlikely to have much impact on their own activities . . .

But the peaceful mood of 1977 was short-lived. By the spring of 1978 it had been succeeded once more by stormy conflict, arising from a desire to produce quick concrete action. One example was the effort made to speed up the housing construction programme.

The building of new homes had been severely delayed due to the continual uncertainty about where to build, and there was now a housing shortage. In discussing the housing construction programme for 1978–1982, people's patience ran out. The opposition demanded that the building start-up in one particular area should be brought forward by a year. After much argument in the executive committee and an extremely lively debate in the council, the opposition's proposal was finally adopted by a large majority, and the council appointed a special unit to ensure that their directives were observed.

This was not the only example. In other cases politicians tried to intervene in negotiations with various external organizations, in order to speed up agreement and consequently actions as well. But such interventions not only weakened the municipality's bargaining position; they also increased internal conflict and delayed action even more.   (Brunsson 1989: 55–6)

This is undoubtedly a story, with characters and a plot: the text is not about 'hotels' or 'public agencies' but about the local government of Runtown in the 1970s. One immediate difference between Thompson's 'illustrations' and Brunsson's 'story' is the volume: Thompson's book is 164 pages long and promises to tackle all the issues in organization theory, Brunsson's has 235 pages and takes up only one specific aspect of it. The character of the 'demonstration' changes: while Thompson's illustrations more or less repeat the proposition on a slightly less abstract level and with more adjectives, Brunsson's story is 'loosely coupled'—to use Weick's terminology, which Brunsson himself also favored—with his general statements, which do not, however, lay claim to any absolute status. In traditional parlance, Thompson's theory is more general, Brunsson's less so; but this is actually quite doubtful. Nobody knows how many concrete cases—if any—Thompson's theory could be applied to, whereas it can be claimed that Brunsson's theory is applicable at least to those cases he studied.

There are, however, some similarities in the demonstration. The Runtown story is a stylized one—not so much because of the avoidance of proper names, which is only to be expected as a way of fulfilling ethical obligations, but because the language is the language of the author and not of the characters. The story of Runtown, in the light of my own knowledge of the Swedish public sector, is a very credible one, but I do not know whether there is 'a' Runtown. It could just as well be a composite[5] of different municipalities and the dramatic fate that they all shared during the late 1970s.

The critique of fiction in scientific texts is often grounded in a confusion of two ways of understanding fiction: as that which does not exist, and that which is not true (Lamarque 1990). If we separate these two, it becomes obvious that Runtown may not exist, and yet everything that is said about it may be true in the above sense—that is, it may be credible in the light of other texts on Swedish municipalities. What I want to emphasize is that stylization intended to raise the 'scientific' timbre of the text tends towards fictionalization. The next two examples either avoid this strategy or push it much further.

STORIES—METAPHORS

Karin D. Knorr Cetina, *The Manufacture of Knowledge: An Essay on the Constructivist and Contextual Nature of Science* (Oxford: Pergamon, 1981).

Knorr Cetina studied one kind of organization—namely, research laboratories, as being large complex organizations in an organization field that is one of the most interconnected in the global economy. Her studies are both exemplary and constitutive of a rapprochement between science and technology studies and organization studies (Latour 1993; Knorr Cetina 1994). On the one hand, sociologists of science and technology began to recognize the organized character of the practices they studied, not least because of the forceful presence of transnational corporations right in the backyard of cozy laboratories. On the other hand, organization students recognized the central role of knowledge production in the organizations they studied (Alvesson 1993). Furthermore, Knorr Cetina's work represents the ethnomethodological influence, which is another increasingly noticeable presence in organization studies (Silverman and Jones 1976; Boden 1994).

---

[5]   Margery Wolf (1992) sees a composite as equivalent to fiction; to Renato Rosaldo (1989), it is a typical device of science and thus the opposite of fiction or at least of narrative.

What follows are excerpts from Knorr Cetina's study of a government-sponsored research center in Berkeley, California.

In the following discussion, I will use the term 'indexicality' to refer to the situational contingency and contextual location of scientific action. This contextual location reveals that the products of scientific research are fabricated and negotiated by particular agents at a particular time and place; that these products are carried by the particular interests of these agents, and by local rather than universally valid interpretations; and that the scientific actors play on the very limits of the situational location of their action. In short, the contingency and contextuality of scientific action demonstrates that the products of science are hybrids which bear the mark of the very indexical logic which characterises their production, and are not the outgrowth of some special scientific rationality to be contrasted with the rationality of social interaction. Scientific method is seen to be much more similar to social method—and the products of natural science more similar to those of social science—than we have consistently tended to assume.

How can we illustrate this indexical logic in somewhat more detail? The first aspect of indexicality is an implied opportunism which manifests itself in a mode of operation comparable to that of a 'tinkerer'. . . . Tinkerers are opportunists. They are aware of the material opportunities they encounter at a given place, and they exploit them to achieve their projects. At the same time, they recognize what is feasible, and adjust or develop their projects accordingly. While doing this, they are constantly engaged in producing and reproducing some kind of workable object which successfully meets the purpose they have temporarily settled on. . . .

As in the example of tinkering, the occasioned character of research first manifests itself in the role played by local resources and facilities. For example, in the institute I observed, the existence of a large-scale laboratory in which proteins could be generated, modified and tested in large volumes was treasured as a valuable opportunity because it would be difficult or impossible to carry out certain kinds of research without such facilities. The laboratory was well equipped, well staffed, and supervised by an experienced older technician described as extremely reliable and 'clever'—a series of additional advantages. As a result, a lot of scientific energy was spent in gaining access to the laboratory in order to 'exploit' this 'resource'. Research which required the use of this laboratory was eagerly sought or invented. A newly purchased electron microscope utilising laser-beams exerted a similar attraction . . .

Preference is also given to technical instruments and apparatus which the scientists know are 'around somewhere'. Projects take certain turns because, as the scientists explain, 'We had a piece of equipment that had been developed in another project that we could use.' Certain measurements are taken because 'the machines were here, so it was very easy to go down and use them', and certain results are obtained because 'well, we were looking for a way to get foam off, you see, and it [the instrument] was there . . ." (Knorr Cetina 1981: 33–5).

The beginning of this extract resembles both Thompson and Brunsson as regards their general statements; the difference is that here the reader can see how metaphors *are manufactured*. They do not just 'show up': the process of choice and construction is revealed in this passage in the example of 'indexicality', which is a richer and more meaningful version of the residual 'environment'. But my main reason for choosing this text was to show a way of connecting stories and metaphors that differs from the previous one and from the one to come: here, metaphors come from stories. What I am saying is that this is a textual strategy that does not depend on the text's immediate order (metaphors come in the text *before* the story), nor does it needs to reflect the author's actual logic. The author presents metaphors as devices that she needs in order to understand, structure, and interpret the stories she has collected/manufactured in the field.

Knorr Cetina takes up a theme not unlike the one mentioned by Thompson in his proposition 4.1: 'organizations' tend to incorporate practices that—people in organizations feel—would leave them vulnerable if left outside. Also, she matches Brunsson by telling stories in an abstract language. But she is running two kinds of story in parallel: those which, allegorically, have metaphors as characters ('tinkerers adjust or develop') and those which have actors (including the author) as characters ('the scientists explain'). In the second kind of story she allowed the actors to speak their own language, achieving the effect of *variegated speech* (Bakhtin 1981). This does not necessarily create an illusion that 'those people' speak for themselves; indeed, it is clear that it was Knorr Cetina who has edited them. Similarly, it is not a matter of 'human touch' or 'focusing on the individual'. The point is very social indeed: the reader becomes aware that different languages and vocabularies are possible and coexistent within one and the same linguistic tradition—a realization much needed in the universalistic language of organization theory (Calás and Smircich 1993).

In her choice of metaphors she shares with Nils Brunsson the influence of US pragmatism: her 'opportunism' resembles his 'hypocrisy', and they both focus on processes rather than structures, showing the way certain things are put to use, rather than stating their existence as Thompson does. A point on which she differs from the first two authors and comes closer to the fourth one below is that she lets 'organization' lose its central place and its metaphorical character. It reacquires its original meaning, that of a state rather than a unit with palpable boundaries. Both she and the next author are interested in forms of social organization in the context of professional practices. This may well herald a more general shift in the way the social processes known as 'organizing' began to be perceived (Weick 1979; Czarniawska 1996).

STORIES AND METAPHORS

Linda Smircich, 'Is the Concept of Culture a Paradigm for Understanding Organizations and Ourselves?', in Peter J. Frost, Larry F. Moore, Mary R. Lewis, Craig C. Lundberg, and Joanne Martin (eds.), *Organizational Culture* (Beverly Hills, Calif.: Sage, 1985), 3–72.

As stated before, the aim behind the present venture and other similar efforts is to collapse the artificial division between science and literature. On the way there is another dichotomy that needs to be collapsed, one that certainly exists although it generally receives less attention: that between the story and the metaphor, or between prose and poetry. This line, useful as it might be for some analytic purposes, such as contrasting rhetoric and poetics (Höpfl 1995), is hard to maintain in analyzing concrete examples of narrative drawn from either theory or practice. It appears that metaphors can support stories or contradict them; stories can disarm metaphors of much of their ambiguity by putting them into a context (Eco 1990); but as a rule they do come together. This can be done, for instance, by letting tropes be characters in the stories, as in the example below.

THE GALAXY TODAY
Archaeology Dig Uncovers Meaning of Corporate Forms
Positive Proof That 'Organization' Is <u>The</u> Paradigm Of Ancient Culture

Planet Earth (UPI)—A major discovery was revealed today (April 1, 3084 AD) by Richard L. S. B. Leakey XII, leader of the Archaeology expedition on the ancient Planet Earth. Leakey, who has been conducting research on the site known as 'Wall Street' for the last 20 years, believes he has at last unlocked the key to understanding the way of life in what is referred to as 'Western Civilization' of the time period 1870–2000 AD.

The Leakey expedition has been searching among the leftovers of life at that time and has recovered an astonishing number of 'computer printouts', 'Xerox machines', 'organization charts', and 'dress for success' books. But these mere artifacts did not provide Leakey with sufficient evidence to confirm his hypothesis about that time period.

In an interview, Leakey said, 'In order for us to make sense of the physical findings we need to uncover a mode of thought, some symbolic connection, between the artifacts. And today we have found it.'

Leakey was referring to a remarkably well-preserved copy of a book by Robert Denhardt, called In the Shadow of Organization, *published in 1981.*

Denhardt's commentary on this civilization called it 'an age of organization'. He characterized society as dominated by an organizational ethic which 'offers itself as a way of life for persons in our society'.

Leakey was visibly excited as he told reporters, 'This book was all I needed to confirm my own theory. These people were crazy for organizations. They valued discipline, order, regulation, and obedience much more than independence, expressiveness and creativity. They were always looking for efficiency. They wanted to control everything. They had a fetish for 'managing'. They managed stress, time, relationships, emotions, but mostly they managed their careers.

'They were somewhat more civilized than the ever more ancient Aztecs. Their sacrifices were bloodless and were conducted on symbolic ladders of success, instead of stone altars.'

Leakey went on to say, 'I'd concluded on my own that these people had a fairly impoverished existence, and this book validates my findings. In the 1980s, organization was the meaning of life. I'll be publishing my findings in Administrative Arts Quarterly, *and will argue conclusively that organization was the paradigm of this culture!'*
(Smircich 1985: 55–6)

How do we know that Smircich's story is a fiction whereas Brunsson's highly fictionalized 'Runtown' was 'the real thing'? Two clues are offered. One is the 'fact' that Smircich includes: the date, 'April 1, 3084 AD'. Another is that Brunsson *tells* the readers that he conducted several studies in the field. As Latour (1988*b*) pointed out, scientific realism differs from fictional realism by the textual strategy of inviting readers to inspect the source of the facts, which most likely contains other references of the same kind; the final loop in the chain then consists in interview transcriptions or some other 'hard data'. I would claim that, had Smircich faked the date (23 August 1984) and claimed a source (participant observation in the Academy of Management Meeting), her claims to scientific realism would weigh much more heavily than Brunsson's, because of her skilful imitation of the rhetoric of the field (it is somewhat unlikely that the Runtown officials would describe their situation in the terms used by Brunsson, whereas it is very likely that an AMA meeting would produce a document like the one quoted by Smircich).

However, even ardent advocates of the narrative mode may nourish a doubt as to whether Smircich's tale is an example of it. There is no chronology that structures the story and, as Ricœur (1984) told us, time and narrative are inseparable. But time *is* a structuring device in Smircich's story, albeit around it, not within it: time (the eleven hundred years difference) is the frame that gives meaning to a speech act reported in the text. Time is a metaphor of distancing. A well-known alternative is that of bringing in 'an observer from Mars', although this also amounts to describing an episode. It was also Ricœur who said that 'the most humble narrative is always more than a chronological series of events, and . . . the configurative dimension cannot eclipse the episoding dimension' (1981: 279). However stylized his episodes, Thompson told stories, too. As soon as even the most formal theory opens itself to examples and illustrations, the narrative enters.[6] Conversely, chronology alone does not create a plot; a sense of closure is most frequently achieved by configurative devices.

In the above paragraph I may be building 'the naïve narrativist' out of straw, but I do not think it is an exaggeration to say that there are many 'anti-narrativists', fond of 'language games', who regard realist narrative with disdain, assuming an inseparable breach between stories and word games. Yet it should be pointed out that all language games are played on the assumption that there is a 'realist narrative' that all readers can easily recognize (and therefore enjoy deviations from it; more about this in the next chapter).

It is less likely, however, that Smircich would be criticized by literary connoisseurs for her tameness than that she would be faulted by followers of the canon—if such exists—for her boldness. In this second perspective there are yet more novelties in Smircich's text. The centrality of the 'organization' metaphor is preserved, but is used ironically: a trope not unknown, but rarely employed in organization theory. A utopian framing is used. Again, this is not

---

[6]   McCloskey (1990*b*) claims that it happens even before; that the most abstract theories are, in fact, stories.

completely unknown in the social sciences, but it is not greatly appreciated (with the possible exception of Habermas and his democratic dialogue), and is used particularly in feminist (i.e. deviant) writings. Thus, to many readers the above text is a breach of the genre on at least three counts: the story is fictitious, irony is used as the main trope, and a utopian frame is applied.

Hence we are back to genre analysis: what happens if (and when) the borders of a genre are crossed?

S/K/TR/ETCHING A GENRE

Fig. 3.3 attempts to summarize the readings above by sketching a space that they seem to create among them. Facts are missing! In the three books (Smircich's is an article) there is only one page solidly filled with facts, and this is the imprint page. Apart from that, facts have an ambiguous position in all these very different works. For Thompson, facts were trite; predictions were more important. Brunsson used 'facts' for framing purposes: we do learn that there was a political crisis in Sweden at the time of his study, and a few other corollaries. The main story—the metaphorical one—is 'loosely coupled' to these facts, and has also been retold in different circumstances (Brunsson and Olsen 1993). Many of Knorr Cetina's facts were 'second hand quotes': they 'belonged' to the scientists she was studying and, as far as her story is concerned, they could have been the exact opposite of what they were. Her visits and observations at the laboratory were facts, but these are important to the reader only as a means of establishing her credibility. Smircich invented her 'facts' entirely.

One clue to this mysterious absence can be found in the introduction to Knorr Cetina's book (1981), where she points out that, etymologically, 'facts' (from *facere*) are basically fabrications, and their production is a speciality of

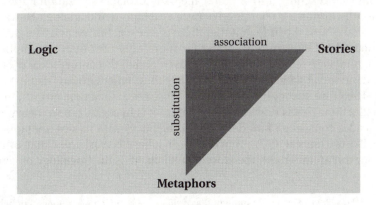

Fig. 3.3. The generic space of organization theory

certain places such as natural-science laboratories. Social scientists seem to be only marginally engaged in fact production; their attention is focused on *how* the facts, and the important societal fictions are produced (Knorr Cetina 1994).

This would bring social science once more closer to literature (see also Lepenies 1988), where the status of facts is quite clear:

Factual judgments as such die as soon as they are transformed into semiotic judgments. Once accepted as true, the factual judgment . . . dies as such in order to generate a stipulation of a code . . . Successful judgments are remembered as such only when they become famous ('the famous discovery of Copernicus' . . .)   (Eco, 1979/1983: 86).

Facts, once known/fabricated, are used in the production of further facts; their repetition does not bring any added value into a discourse. Metaphors, on the other hand, 'tend to resist acquisition. If they are inventive (and thus original) they cannot be easily accepted; the system tends not to absorb them' (Eco 1979/1983: 86). Once accepted, they become redundant, and lose their attraction. Stories, on the other hand, are allowed to be redundant: a narrative of a redundant nature, says Eco defending detective stories, offers a fastidious reader an opportunity to repose, to relax. Thus the combination of stories and metaphors seems to be irresistible, but at the same time seemingly puts an end to the genre of organization studies, which vanishes into literature.

Margery Wolf, whose work inspired the title of the present chapter,[7] is one of many social scientists who worry about 'how one is to differentiate ethnography from fiction, other than in preface, footnotes, and other authorial devices' (1992: 56). I note this standing concern, but fail to appreciate its gravity, and I try to justify my levity in the chapter that follows. However, I do share her concern for specificity. What can be said to be specific to social-science writing, and especially to organization studies—at least in terms of frequent use if not of intrinsic characteristics? Is there any 'core' to this genre?

The picture above has been composed as a combination of McCloskey's tetrad and the four texts reviewed here. Metaphors and stories are the basis of the space so created. While the methods of association tend towards logic without ever reaching it (one could speak of a 'logical stylization'), the methods of substitution are contained between metaphor and analogy. However, in genre analysis, or the little of it that there is (see e.g. Burrell and Morgan 1979), the methods of substitution attract far more attention than the methods of association. One reason could be that the eighteenth-century ideal of science landed the social sciences in a country of *things*, where nouns (names) matter most. Therefore, the methods of substitution, not association, attract attention and reflection. This is nowhere clearer than it is in organization theory, which for decades consisted of models containing boxes with names (metaphors) in them, like the ones at the bottom of Fig. 3.1. It has been assumed that, once you get your metaphors right, the story will tell itself. If the 'sociology of verbs' as

---

[7]   *A Thrice-Told Tale.* I must point out that Wolf, too, tells her story four times, but has better reasons than I for keeping the alliteration in the title intact.

postulated by John Law (1994) ever takes hold, however, the obscure arrows standing for vague connections, as in 'it causes', 'it influences', or 'it relates to', will become the focus of social science. Causes how? Influences by what means? As Dvora Yanow (1996) provocatively asks, 'How does a policy mean?' Reflection upon the modes of association has yet to be developed in the texts of the social sciences in general and organization theory in particular.

Within the space above, a typical mode of association would be such parallel storytelling as is exemplified by the works of Brunsson and Knorr Cetina: a 'story from the field' retold in an allegorical way, with metaphors as the main characters and narrative exchanged for logic. None of them will do on their own: a logical-metaphorical tale must be translatable to some place and space, and, although traditionally social-science authors have expected the readers to do the job, it makes much more sense if they do it themselves, saving the readers from wild attempts at 'validation' and the legitimation of their abstract tales all at once.

What about the works that are at the edge the genre so defined? Is Thompson 'out', as belonging to another convention? Is Smircich threatening the genre with her innovations? It is tempting to ask and answer such questions. Genre construction is institution-building, and as such it invites policing attempts: somebody must 'protect the core'. As genre analysis in literature has shown, however, such protective policing leads to the suffocation of a genre in the worst case and to nothing in the best—as Lejeune (1989) pointed out, criticizing Northrop Frye for his genre-policing. However, the analysis of a genre is one of the genre's constitutive forces. As social scientists, we busy ourselves constructing the institutions we describe. Neither paradoxicality nor conflict weakens a genre; on the contrary, they enhance its controlling power. And among the authors who operate in the gray zones are innovators: those who rejuvenate and reform the genre.

One such innovation, hinted at in Smircich's text and developed by Latour (1996) for example, is a text that mixes the two kinds of tale: the logical analysis alternates with a story, and they are kept together by common metaphors. The 'theory' provides the plot and builds the suspense. After all, a plot is 'the conceptual structure which binds the events of a story together . . . Plots are not events, but structures of events' (Bernstein 1990: 55). One way, represented by Brunsson and Knorr Cetina, is to tell the structure and then tell the story: to tell the story twice, on different levels of abstraction. Another, illustrated by Smircich, is to make the structure deducible from the story. This is a device common in literature and unusual in social science. What is being recommended here is not replacing one genre by another, not writing fiction instead of social science: it is creative borrowing. 'Hybridizing the genre' would perhaps be a fitting expression.

To the few wooden tongues developed in academic journals, we should add the many genres and styles of narration invented by novelists, journalists, artists, cartoonists, scientists and philosophers. The reflexive character of our domain will be recognized in the future by the multiplicity of genres, not by the tedious presence of 'reflexive loops'. (Latour 1988*a*: 173).

What Margery Wolf says of anthropology could be applied to all social sciences, but especially to management. Management too 'is a discipline with very permeable borders, picking up methodologies, theories, and data from any source whatever that can provide the answers to our questions' (Wolf 1992: 51). All these 'loans' arrive in packages typical of the genre from which they have come. Traditionally, however, social scientists tended to ignore 'the form', insisting that it is the 'pure contents' that are being tapped.[8] Latour's advice amounts to a suggestion to make a virtue out of a vice, an art out of an unreflective behavior.

---

[8] Simmel's lecture 'The Picture Frame' (1902/1994) made me think that 'form' and 'content' were treated in the social sciences exactly (and misleadingly) like 'frame' and 'picture', two separate entities rather than two inseparable aspects of the same thing.

4

Realism in the Novel, Social Sciences, and Organization Theory

The idea that scientific and non-scientific writing might have something in common is neither especially remarkable nor particularly new. The very fact that so much effort has been invested into differentiating art from science since Plato's *Republic* would suggest a proximity that was disquieting—at least to some audiences who demanded a clearer demarcation between the two. At the same time, there were always voices like that of Giambattista Vico, intent on abolishing this difference. Anyone keen on periodization as a sensemaking device would be able to discern periods when one or the other school of thought was in ascendance.

One such period worth mentioning is the early eighteenth century, when modern natural sciences began to assume their present shape. In Schaffer's rendition of those 'Augustan Realities' (1993), scientists such as Isaac Newton and Jeremy Bentham did tremendous 'cultural work', gaining legitimacy for their science through committed political writing and public spectacles, of which the most spectacular example was the autopsy of Bentham's body performed, at his request, in the presence of his friends at his house. This part of history is relatively well known; what attracts less attention is the meta-activity of erasing the traces of artistry and politics from their work, the accomplishment of having established a genre of scientific realism as 'a philosophical position that distracts attention from this cultural work of representatives of nature, and points it toward the adequacy of nature's representations . . . the "amnesia" of realism, in which the work that establishes representations is forgotten' (Schaffer 1993: 279).

The realistic style has earned a legitimate place in both genres: in scientific realism and in the Realist novel. Some more work was thus needed to establish the difference between the two, and especially between the Realist novel and the social sciences, which both emerged at about the same time in the nineteenth century. This time around, the legitimizing efforts were directed not only at establishing each of them as genres in their own right, but also at distinguishing between what initially looked very much alike.

The years 1950–70, exploiting the scientific contributions to the Second World War, brought another wave of 'scientization' to social sciences (Lepenies 1988). The late 1970s, however, witnessed what is often called a 'linguistic turn' in the social sciences, which was soon accompanied by a 'literary turn'. Examples abound: the rhetorical analysis in economics (McCloskey 1986) and in most of the social sciences and humanities (Nelson *et al.* 1987), the reconstruction of the burnt bridges between sociology and literary theory (Bakhtin/Medvedev 1928/1985; Brown 1977; Bruss 1982; Lepenies 1988; Agger 1990), the knitting of close ties between anthropology and literary theory (Geertz 1973, 1988; Marcus and Fischer 1986), and the ongoing debate about the importance of narrative knowledge, summarized in Chapter 2.

THE NOVEL AND THE SOCIAL SCIENCES: THE COMMON BEGINNINGS

When Auguste Comte was developing his positive science of sociology, few of his admirers were so ardent as Émile Zola, who considered his work the embodiment of the new scientific ideal.[1] Little did he know that, in times to come, he would be judged as unscientific by the scientists and as non-literary by the *literati*. This judgement, however, was issued much later, when Positivism had separated itself from the 'humanities' in the pursuit of true science. The beginnings were different.

The Age of Realism was the age of railways and of wireless telegraphy and of countless other mechanical inventions that collectively revolutionized the nature of society and the quality of human life within a short span of time. It was the age during which what used to be called 'natural philosophy' was rechristened 'science', having finally ridded itself of the few shreds of speculative idealism that still adhered to it. It was the age of the expansion of Europe into Asia and Africa, after which the legendary 'terra incognita' disappeared from the atlases. It was the age of nationalism and rampant commercialism, but also the age when international revolutionary movements began to threaten the security of the wealthy governing classes.   (Hemmings 1978*a*: 9)

Hemmings traces the earliest recorded use of the word 'realism' to *Le Mercure français*, which, in 1826, wrote about 'a literary doctrine . . . which would lead to the imitation not of artistic masterpieces but of the originals that nature offers us . . . the literature of truth' (Hemmings 1978*a*: 9–10). In April of the same year, Comte began a series of lectures on a 'system of positive philosophy'. Both doctrines aimed at a representation *corresponding* to the world as it was—undistorted by any subjective or partial vision.

Within the world of literature, this Promethean task was not seen as particularly formidable: the fear was that dullness and boredom would be the result.

---

[1] The following three sections are based on my essay 'Realism in Novel, Social Sciences and Organization Theory' published in Czarniawska-Joerges and Guillet de Monthoux (1994: 304–23).

Writers, used to the 'running-commentary' technique à la Richardson, could not see the point of an unemotional relation of the facts of life 'as they were'. However, when put into practice, the principle itself proved untenable:

All through the 'age of realism' novelists will be faced with the same dilemma: social institutions, human relationships, the separate courses of individual lives, all these cannot be presented in a work of art without a certain measure of trimming and tailoring . . . However firm his allegiance to realism, a novelist has to impose his own peculiar vision on what he sees, partly because this vision is inseparable from his artistic consciousness, and partly because without it his work would lack shape and point and would finally prove unreadable.   (Hemmings 1978a: 33)

This dilemma attracted the attention of social scientists much later: unused to reflecting upon their research and writing, only since the 1980s have they begun to ponder over the paradoxes of 'objectivity' and 'correspondence theory of truth'. But the novelists were not only ahead of the social scientists in their self-reflectivity, they were also ahead in reaching the wider public. Comte (1798–1857) formulated the Positivist program; it was not until Durkheim (1858–1917) that this program was applied to societal problems.

Throughout the nineteenth century it was still the novelists and historians who were *describing* the formation of mature capitalism. The economists, such as Smith and Malthus, were laying the foundation of a *normative* science, under the aegis of moral philosophy or causal laws. The science (art?) of business and public administration, with its peculiar mixture of economic and sociological methods and interests, did not yet exist; the realist novel was its close approximation.

This statement must be qualified in relation to specific contexts. Literary Realism and its radical version, Naturalism, were born in France and adopted in countries under direct French literary influence, such as Poland and Portugal. Other countries, with competing literary cultures, reacted in more complex ways. In Russia, Realism was never far removed from Symbolism, as illustrated by the debate on Dostojevsky's *Dead Souls*, focusing 'the necessary paradoxical character of all realism in literature, how it presumes to reflect a reality that needs be apprehended subjectively by a writer who has nothing more adequate than language with which to objectify his own version of the real' (Freeborn 1978: 90). This multilayered Realism aimed at reflection of societal developments that still contained only early and primitive forms of the use of capital. Financial and industrial organizations usually belonged to foreigners and, when serving as topic for novelists, were used to show how they clashed with the host culture.

In Germany, on the other hand, the Realists kept to a 'village tale', as a kind of opposition to industrialization, which they disliked and distrusted. This reaction was embedded in the intellectual life of Germany at the beginning of the nineteenth century. The Realist novel, condemned as a typical expression of the nascent bourgeois society, was not popular among German writers. In Germany writing and reading were traditionally solitary acts, and literature that concerned itself with matters of society had always been counted superficial and 'non-German'. In contrast, poetry was given a special place in German culture (Lepenies 1988).

In Spain, the main trend was that of *naturalismo*, considered by some to be a synonym of Realism, by others a crude variation of Realism, but by most as 'a conscious attempt to apply to literature the discoveries and methods of nineteenth-century science, particularly the biological sciences' (Rutherford and Hemmings 1978: 284). Emilia Pardo Bazán (1851–1921) analyzed this trend, and found Zola wanting, especially in his allegiance to Darwinism, which was difficult for a Catholic audience to accept. Pardo Bazán postulated the supremacy of an all-inclusive, objective Realism based on testable laws, and not untestable speculations (like those concerning evolution). This postulate reflects the progress of the Positivist program, which more and more clearly saw itself as free from 'fiction' of any kind. As Hemmings put it, they had 'no interest in weakening the force of their findings by wrapping them up in the distracting packaging of art' (Hemmings 1978*b*: 302).

In Italy, Angelo Camillo De Mais (1817–1891), Professor of the History of Medicine at the University of Bologna, expressed his opinion on Realism as follows: 'The novel of science, the extraordinary story of reason: can there be a more absurd combination? Of course not.' (Carsaniga 1978: 344–5). And, although there were Italian Realists describing the emerging world of organizations (see Manoukian 1994), De Mais's opinion became general by the 1890s. The novel returned to Romanticism, science moved towards Positivism. The following epitaph, although written in 1978, gives a good summary of the feelings prevailing at the turn of the previous century:

Long before Zola proclaimed the novelist to be a social scientist, his predecessors had been dignifying their activities by using scientific terminology to describe them: they claimed to be writing *studies* rather than works of imaginative fiction; they *analysed* social problems; they collected data by diligent enquiry and *research* . . . in all this they were doing no more than duplicating in an amateurish sort of way those who were . . . laying the foundations of twentieth-century academic sociology. (Hemmings 1978*b*: 362)

It is either historical justice or a historical irony that the end of the next century again sees scientists (not only social) dignifying their activities by an amateurish (that is, loving) duplication of the rhetoric of literary criticism. By joining this effort, I hope to help to avenge Zola. It might be appropriate to quote George Bernard Shaw, who commented on Zola's work in a letter to Augustin Hamon in 1910:

Zola was vulgar; Zola had no humour, Zola had no style. Yet he was head and shoulders above contemporaries of his who had refinement, wit and style to a quite exquisite degree. The truth is that what determines a writer's greatness is neither his accomplishments nor the number of things he knows by observation; but solely his power of perceiving the relative importance of things. (Shaw 1971: 914)

ROMANTICISM AND POSITIVISM AS DOUBLE RHETORIC OF MODERNITY

From the point of view of literary history, Romanticism could be seen as a literary phenomenon of the early eighteenth century, preceding Realism, which was followed by Symbolism. In the following discussion, however, I wish to present Romanticism as a habit of mind,[2] or a rhetoric, that can be contrasted with Positivism (R. H. Brown 1980; 1987; 1989). Together, they constitute the two main rhetorics of modernity. Representing opposite stances produces a tension that guarantees dramatic results for the audience, but a closer look reveals that the two rhetorics not only contradict but also complement each other.

In the Positivist version of scientific realism, for example, society and individual became separated from one another. The individual became part of a cybernetic system, ruled by laws uninfluenced by will or personal history. Reality and knowledge became the sole domain of positive science, which offered guidance in all matters relevant to society. 'Science has emerged as a kind of religion, an ultimate frame of reference for determining what is real and true' (R. H. Brown 1980: 548). Experts appropriated the public voice, leaving lay persons an illusory choice between exit (into individual privacy) and loyalty, to borrow Hirschman's (1977) phrase. 'Public' as a term was slowly changing its meaning from denoting the informed citizenry collectively making its decisions to mean that experts' opinions are publicly known, rather than reserved for the powerful only. Judgements of good and evil were replaced by estimations of profit or political expediency, moral evaluation of people, and the results of their actions by calculating their utility (as in the human-resources tradition or in social accounting). Additionally, while officially rejecting rhetoric, Positivism developed a new vocabulary: that of scientific rationality, particularly systems theory. The two mastertropes of this rhetoric were the Baconian 'objectivity' and the Cartesian 'causality'.

This reified—and reifying—picture of reality, where moral agency had no part to play, met with violent opposition from Romanticism. Unlike the protagonists of the early Realist novel, where society was a vehicle for an individual, the Romantic heroes and heroines fulfilled what they saw as their moral duty against the law of society, and often at the cost of their lives. Those who still tried to achieve harmony between the public and the private, were condemned to absurdity, as in Kafka. One kind of Romantic protest expressed itself in a search for peak experiences—as rebellion against the institutionalization of the self, a way out that was propagated in high culture by poets such

---

[2] The concept 'refers to those societal or epochal structures of consciousness that provide the ordering principles for accounts in everyday life' (Brown 1989: 9). See also Bourdieu's (1977) concept of *habitus*.

as Rimbaud and Byron, much as in today's New Age low culture. Another kind of protest is represented in Kundera's *The Art of the Novel* (1988), which re-establishes the romantic quest for the European spirit—'an imaginative realm of tolerance'—within 'the wisdom of the novel'.

A way of thinking trying to reach beyond the agonistic dualism of Romanticism and Positivism adopts a diacritical rather than a dialectical point of view. From such a vantage point, the two antithetical perspectives do not contribute to a higher-level synthesis, but simply acquire meaning through the difference between them (R. H. Brown 1989). Romantics needed the bour-geoisie in order to shock them by repudiating their ideals. Rebels need a well-defined social order to rebel against. Similarly, a system that produces and thrives on Positivist reality and knowledge creates both the need and the possi-bility of emotional safety valves in the form of organizational rituals, vicarious peak experiences in mass media, and so on.

What is more, the two antagonists find themselves immobilized in the deadlock of a language of extremes. While some authors on both sides never tire of fencing with the old clichés, their audiences become more and more disenchanted—be it on aesthetic or moral grounds. Brown sees a forced choice—between bureaucratized social life and alienating private with-drawal—as denying the possibility of both individual moral action and collec-tive public discourse. In this, the two alleged enemies surreptitiously join forces to form a duopoly of modern discourse. Rorty (1989) called it 'a cultural hegemony'.

The disenchantment led, among other things, to challenging the barriers between science and 'the arts', including science and the novel. Science ought to be dealing with 'an outer world of things', and the arts with 'an inner world of choice' (R. H. Brown, 1987: 162), but neither Positivist science nor the Romantic novel was able to delineate the frontier between the two. This becomes more understandable in the light of a growing recognition that both 'worlds' belong to the same socially constructed system of symbols.

The two domains—the social sciences and the novel—reacted to this ques-tioning of old dualisms separately but in parallel. A new kind of criticism emerged in the literary realm, a criticism that rejected both the objectivist determinism of Positivism and the subjectivist humanism of Romanticism. The social sciences underwent a similar process of self-reflection, which was as much influenced by developments in literary criticism as it was (and still is) by developments in natural sciences. A truly post-Positivist and post-Romantic discourse has yet to develop, concluded R. H. Brown, who himself, following Bakhtin's lead, had already proposed *A Poetic for Sociology* in 1977. In search-ing for such a discourse, social sciences and the novel met again. Let us trace some of the forms that this encounter takes, and the implication it has for the scientific paradigm and the literary style both known as realism.

Although literary Realism was conventionally associated with Positivism rather than with Romanticism, if we assume that the Romantic and Positivist rhetorics evolved in close relation to each other, Realism must also be seen as connected to both of them and their common fate. Indeed, one could claim that the Realist novel never properly learned to differentiate between the two. From its beginnings, it celebrated holism as the only proper perspective on both society and the individual. It celebrated individualism but in a framework of society that was the proper field for personal praxis. This tradition survived in the US novels about self-made heroes and heroines, a kind of narrative that came to be considered naive within both Positivist and Romanticist traditions. This kind of narrative presupposed, as a scene on which public action by moral agents could unfold, a stable social order, a clear-cut political economy, and a collective psychology in which personal character and public conduct were assumed to be inseparable. When such assumptions became untenable, some proclaimed 'the end of the novel'. Others, such as Tom Wolfe and Malcolm Bradbury, announced a revival of the Realist novel. Indeed, although the meaning of 'realist' might change, there are no indications that the form is anything but thriving. If this is so, it should open opportunities for renewed encounters between the novel and this other realist genre: the social sciences.

NATURALISM AND CRITICAL REALISM

The notion of a paradigm shift (from Positivism to, let us say, post-Positivism) has attracted so much attention since the 1980s that it would be superfluous to repeat it here. I have chosen here to sample two versions of an emerging approach—naturalism and critical realism—because both are relevant for organization studies, and because they appreciate the value of realist reporting while avoiding naïve assumptions about iconic correspondence between words and non-words, between knowledge and the world.

Of the two, naturalism, true to tradition, is the more radical. Although the name pays its historical debt, it is clear that this time we have to do with a 'social nature' and the kind of realism espoused is all but naïve (the paradigm is also called a 'naturalistic hermeneutics' (Manicas and Rosenberg 1988)).

Guba (1985) attempted to formulate the basic tenets of this approach for the use of organization studies. To begin with, there are many constructions of reality (thus many realities) that will always lead to divergent enquiry results. Therefore, the outcomes of a scientific enquiry can contribute much to an increased understanding, not to prediction and control. This is much like *belles lettres*. Also, there is no obvious border between a 'subject' and an 'object' of research, the objects being human and therefore subjects themselves. Enquiry is an interaction. Knowledge is idiographic in character—attempts at nomothetic descriptions of the human world are in vain. Social phenomena are overdetermined (a Freudian notion applied to organization theory by Weick 1979) and fruitless efforts at establishing simple causality should be abandoned in favor of detecting patterns of actions, events, processes. There is never a single answer to the question why an organization changed as it did, but there are illuminating and instructive ways of describing how it changed when it did. Finally, all enquiry is inextricably value laden (a sobering acknowledgment on the part of the scientists, not the least because this was supposedly the decisive difference between science and non-science).

Lincoln, elaborating the consequences of the program sketched by Guba, pointed out that the 'case-study reporting mode'—that is, the one closest to a traditional novelistic narrative—might serve the emergent approach best (Lincoln 1985).

Interestingly enough, the 'new naturalists' seem to share a tendency to exaggerate with their literary predecessors. In particular, their ways of achieving trustworthiness lead both to painstaking research audits (Skrtic 1985), where 'human instruments' were checked and controlled, and to a difficulty of political reflection in the light of the fact that the 'member check' was made the final authority (i.e. the actors in the field have to accept a report for it to be trustworthy).

Critical realism[3] in contrast to Positivism but in company with other contemporary trends in philosophy (see the next section) explicitly acknowledged its proximity to *belles lettres* and often trespassed on its grounds, not the least in the conscious use of hermeneutic methods. It avoids the pitfalls of naturalism but encounters some other problems.

Critical realists assume that social life emerged from nature, and therefore both nature and society are constituted and constrained although not reducible to the laws of causal determination. Having made this claim, they maintain traditional realism's ambition of discovering and describing these causal laws, and they reject idealistic influences by indicating that 'all social existence has an irremediably "material" dimension, located in space and time, and expressed through material engagements with a world' (Isaac 1990: 5). Organizations may be conceived as symbolic systems, but they should be conceived as tools for changing the material reality.

Unlike traditional realists, critical realists see knowledge as a social and historical product, and social life as symbolic. They hasten, however, to add—in order to protect themselves from a dangerous proximity to social constructivism—that social life is not reducible to the concepts and meanings of the actors, who draw on pre-existing configurations ('social structures').[4] They make concessions to social constructivism by admitting that these structures are constantly reinterpreted and renegotiated, and are subject to historical transformation. Nevertheless, 'the task of generalizing,

---

[3] I adopt the term used by Isaac (1990), whose insightful discussion I am going to relate at some length. Critical realism is also a term used to describe fiction, where Turgenev and Conrad are the most quoted examples. The authors to whom this perspective is attributed include Bhaskar (e.g. Bhaskar, 1989), Harré (who calls his variety of realism a 'referential realism' (Harré, 1986)), Manicas (who uses terms such as 'conventional' or 'single-barrelled' realism (see e.g. Manicas and Rosenberg 1988)).

[4] The evils of social constructivism vary from one critic to another. While a typical attack accuses social constructivists of propagating a conservative, apologetic stance (if we are the constructors of reality, we must like it), the critical realists accuse them of luring people into believing that the change is all too easy (see Giddens 1990; 1991).

explanatory social theory is to analyze the properties of such structures, as media and outcomes of human practice' (Isaac 1990: 6) and not, as social constructivists would have it, the very process of production and reproduction of these structures.

The assumptions of 'critical realism' can attract many people—writers, social scientists, and management theorists alike (Alvesson and Willmott 1992). The attractive part is its softened epistemological assumption (knowledge is contained in stories), but its attempt to expurgate the specter of relativism by firmly sticking to a causally structured reality leads to problems. Fay (1990), introducing the metaphor of cartography, showed why this strategy of keeping the cake and eating it, filled by an unavoidable tension, is not really necessary.

In cartography there is a terrain mapmakers want to map, and they devise various modes of projection by which to represent the various aspects of this terrain. (Indeed, there are no contours of the terrain as such, independently of any mode of representing them. The terrain is an entity in part constituted by some form of representation or other.) Of course, what aspects of the terrain they will map will in part be the result of where and how they look at it—at what level, so to speak, they perceive it (maps of the earth drawn from the perspective of the moon will look quite different from ones drawn from the perspective of the earth itself). Also, which mode of representation is employed will be a result of what it is that they want to represent, and for what purposes. There is no 'One Best Map' of a particular terrain. For any terrain there will be an indefinite number of useful maps, a function of the indefinite levels and kinds of description of the terrain itself, as well as the indefinite number of modes of representations and uses to which they can be put.   (Fay 1990: 37)

Observe that the notion of 'terrain' does not exclude the 'objective' existence of earth—on the contrary, it assumes it. What it refuses is the 'correspondence'—even as a 'rough ideal of adequacy' (Manicas, quoted in Isaac 1990: 5). Borges in his *Historia universal de la infamia* mockingly recounted the story of a map that was identical with the country it represented—leading to the end of the discipline of cartography in the country ('Del rigor en la ciencia'). A scientific description that equals what it describes is an absurdity. 'Realism' must mean something else, and both naturalism and critical realism try to construct it.

What are the possible uses—or misuses—of naturalism and critical realism in organization studies? The methodological antics of naturalism do not contribute to an understanding of contemporary organizations, but its main aim—to study people in their 'natural' setting rather than in the sterile environment of thought-up models—is important. Critical realism, on the other hand, scrutinizes the philosophical issues that can provide material for a crucial kind of reflection: what do we study? what do we present as a study report? Both schools of thought recommend realism as the reporting mode for scientific studies. The advice can be taken directly into studies of organizations. Consequently, we need to take literature more seriously in order to perfect our own genre.

AN EDIFYING CONVERSATION?

While realist philosophy is still largely occupied with counting (epistemo-logical) angels on the head of an (ontological) pin, literature takes greater liber-ties. Kundera (1988: 32) claims that this was always the case: 'The novel dealt with the unconscious before Freud, the class struggle before Marx, it practised phenomenology . . . before the phenomenologists.' Bakhtin explained this 'prescience of the novelists' by the artists' 'keen sense for ideological problems in the process of birth and generation', which is often keener than that of 'the more cautious "man of science", the philosopher, or the technician' (Bakhtin/Medvedev 1928/1985: 17). Instead of dropping Realism in the face of growing critique, the Realist novel incorporated the critique itself.

Thus it can be said that the novel accepted and understood the paradox-icality of social life before the postmodern thinkers did. Gabriel Garcia Marquez trained his readers to accept the intricacies of magic realism, where it became even more clear that old dualisms of materialism–idealism and involvement–detachment could no longer be sustained. When Umberto Eco and Salman Rushdie described the present and the past, our own and exotic cultures, it became possible to accept the lack of clear boundaries. Writers of my generation—Paul Auster, Julian Barnes, William Boyd, Patrick Süskind, and Jeanette Winterson—seem to reach beyond modernism and postmodernism, both modernist inventions, to the country of last things, which does not yet have a name, but which maintains realistic appearances.

Their kind of realism accepts the fact that, not only works of art, but all re-presentations, add to reality rather than repeat it. Only the easily scared are still shaking their heads over Goodman's (1978) 'irrealist' claim that we are all world-makers. Examples of perspectives that parallel the literary develop-ments are Brown's (1977) 'poetic for sociology' and Richard Rorty's pragmatism (Rorty 1980; 1982, 1989). Rorty's position is interesting in so far as it avoids the self-imposed problems of critical realism and it seems directly applicable to the studies of organizations.

First, the realist ontology is moved into the realm of belief. It is sensible and convenient to *believe* in the world of causes 'out there'; after all, the organiza-tional actors base all their professional existence on such an assumption. To organize, to manage, to undertake—all this requires a faith that there is a world of causes and that people can be agents in the world. This does not mean, however, that there are ways of describing this world that correspond to it 'as it really is'.

To say that the world is out there, that it is not our creation, is to say, with common sense, that most things in space and time are the effects of causes which do not include human mental states. To say that truth is not out there is simply to say that where there are no sentences there is no truth, that sentences are elements of human languages, and that human languages are human creations.   (Rorty 1989: 4–5)

Secondly, as I mentioned in Chapter 1, the superior notion of *episteme* (knowledge) becomes identical with *doxa* (opinion), until now held in disrepute by science (Rorty 1991*a*). Organizational actors have opinions on all kinds of matters and test them in action. Pragmatism is a philosophy meant for people of action; it is a kind of theory that explores practices rather than explains principles.

Social science is thus a kind of writing, and its various disciplines can be best compared to literary genres. Therefore it should be only natural that organization theory, as a genre, engages in a conversation with other genres. The present book is intended as an illustration and an attempt to persuade readers that such a conversation is possible and desirable.

In such a perspective, novels are sources not of information, but of meaning. They are texts to be taken into account while other texts are produced; models—not for imitation, but for inspiration. They are versions of the world, and, in so far as these are relevant and valid, it is not by virtue of correspondence with 'the world', but by the virtue of containing right ('entrenched') categories and of being acceptable (Goodman 1984). Such versions of worlds gain acceptability, not in spite of, but because of, their aesthetic features. It is the power of creative insight and not documentary precision that makes novels both a potential competitor and a dialogue partner for organization theory.

Were such a conversation to start, would organization theory not find itself in the role of pupil rather than teacher? Kundera (1988: 64) claimed for the novel an 'extraordinary power of incorporation: whereas neither poetry nor philosophy can incorporate the novel, the novel can incorporate both poetry and philosophy without losing thereby anything of its identity, which is characterized . . . precisely by its tendency to embrace other genres, to absorb philosophical and scientific knowledge'.

Is there a danger that, with such a teacher, all organization researchers become novelists? Hardly. After all, the analogy between novelists and organization researchers is only an analogy, and as such has its limits. Also, an organization researcher is in many respects more a literary critic than a novelist. The organizations that the researchers describe are only in a certain sense products of their mind (in the sense that they are responsible for their own texts); the organizations are originally written by organizational actors. They, like the literary authors, have quite a lot to say about the critics' opinions of their production. Organization researchers work on an uncertain footing, in so far as they undertake mediation between the 'organizational authors' and the academic theorists. The latter, however, meet their colleagues pursuing the theory of literature on a similar level, and the experiences between theory-makers can be exchanged on a more equal footing.

AN APOLOGY TO REFLECTIVE REALISM

If the analogy between novelists and organization researchers can be accepted in spite all its limitations, a question still remains whether, with so many genres in existence, Realism is a good teacher to learn from. There seems to exist a contradiction between pragmatism's refutation of the 'mirror-of-the-mind' metaphor of science (Rorty 1980) and literary realism's eager espousal of it. But these are two different mirrors. When Stendhal said that 'a novel is a mirror riding along a highway' (Levin 1973: 66), he could not have had in mind 'the notion of knowledge as inner representation' (Rorty 1980: 46). Mirrors are also versions of worlds.

One could say, with the critics of literary realism, that novelists simply got the precepts of science wrong. Alternatively, one can join the critics of scientism in claiming that it is literature that offers a better insight into the social character of human cognition. The difference is located elsewhere: 'the world of one single Truth and the relative, ambiguous world of the novel are molded of entirely different substances' (Kundera 1988: 14). A good novel makes the readers believe in its worlds by the force of persuasion (just like good science), not by the force of external authority.

Realism is one way of world-making that was selected for inspection here because it employs the rhetoric closest to that of our own discipline. As Latour (1988b) points out, one common device used to build up an impression of 'reality representation' is by alluding to the fact that the authors possess 'evidence' supporting what they say. Scientific realism is characterized by the fact that the authors mobilize the documents within the text (tables, graphs, references). Additionally, the reader is promised a possibility of checking on these documents (by, say, a visit to a laboratory, author's office, or library). Indeed, the journalists who interview researchers at their office tend to believe that their computers 'contain the data'. The novelists understood this technique long ago and used it for their own purposes (as, for instance, in Jean d'Ormesson's *The Glory of the Empire* (1971), complete with footnotes, page references, and all).

Although the debates on realism—in science and in literature—continue, there is a growing consensus on understanding the concept in the way indicated above: not as a 'way of writing corresponding to reality' but as a 'way of writing corresponding to the contemporary criteria of realist writing' (Levine 1993). The main issue is then an institutionalized preference for a given style of writing over another.

Accordingly, realism is but one literary style that offers insights into social reality, but a sturdy one. A British writer and literary theorist, Malcolm Bradbury, in a discussion with the US writer Tom Wolfe, said that the reason for realism or a form of it had in his opinion never really gone away, and that 'our modernist, post-modernist and therefore presumably anti-realist century' enjoys it perhaps more than ever (Bradbury 1992: 17).

This claim can be extended beyond the novel and into the social sciences ending with organization theory. One would think that, with the arrival of constructivism, relativism, and postmodernism, realism would have been banned once and for all. Far from it—it proliferates as perhaps never before. Within philosophy, there is the scientific realism of Rom Harré and the critical realism of Mary Hesse and Roy Bhaskar, promising to reconcile constructivism and realism. Sociology is not left behind: there is the symbolic realism of Richard H. Brown, the conventional realism of Peter Manicas, the social-science realism of Andrew Sayer, and the 'real-ism' of David Silverman and Brian Torode. In anthropology, Bruno Latour and Clifford Geertz have discussed how to achieve a realist effect without getting trapped in naïve realism.

For organization theorists, realism may be the most attractive style in which to present their knowledge, because it is both legitimate and expected. The question is then not 'Whether realism' but 'What kind of realism?'.

There are many demands for realism in stories about organizations and they are serious, but not very specific. Stern (1973: 40) listed three ways of understanding realism in literature and literary critique: 'A way of depicting, describing the situation in a faithful, accurate, "life-like" manner; or richly, abundantly, colourfully; or again mechanically, photographically, imitatively.' It is against the third and in favor of the second of these interpretations of realism that the present appeal is made. A realist study does not have to denote the naïve simplicity of the 'it-is-true-because-I-was-there' kind of realism. Let me give some examples of works that, in my opinion, avoid such traps of naïve realism.

A SUBGENRE OF ERGONOGRAPHY?

One possible subgenre in organization studies, the one that combines insights coming from literary theory with an anthropological frame of mind, could be called *ergonography* or a realist version of organizational ethnography (Czarniawska 1997).

'Ergonography' is obviously a neologism that I coined partly for political reasons—to differentiate a genre that is typical of the kind of studies I am propagating—and partly for etymological reasons, in the sense that other possible candidates have an etymological past that make them less suitable.

What I mean is 'ethnographies of organizing'. The *graphon* (Gr.) part remains where it is: it is clear that our business is to write, but it is unclear what we should write. The adjective *ethno* has a somewhat complicated history. In ethnology it means (by use, not by definition) studying what people do when they do not organize. While one may argue that the thus-defined topic of ethnology might wither with time (see Perrow 1991 on the society of organizations), at present the problem is just that the word 'ethnography' seems to suggest the opposite of what organization researchers are doing. Ethnomethodology is, in fact, the closest term, but its emphasis on 'method' is deceptive.

Ergon is a Greek word meaning work, but akin to *organon*, instrument. It is worth remembering that it is not organisms that are metaphors for organizations; it is organizations that became (long, one can guess, before organization theory) metaphors for organisms. Working as organizing is indeed the topic of management and organization theory.

One type of ergonographies represents what can be called an *ironic realism*: Robin Leidner's (1993) study is one example, Gideon Kunda's (1992) another. Kunda's work contained a series of mini-narratives illustrating life in Tech (the fictive name of the corporation) that remained in ironic contradiction to one another. This irony was not of Kunda's making: it proved to be the way of life (and survival) at Tech. The truly skilful operators of Tech's predominant ideology shifted effortlessly between the mode of total commitment and the mode of detached irony, including self-irony. Tech was a subtle 'culture trap', and its members lived the truly postmodern life of spectators at an everlasting spectacle of which they wanted to be directors at the same time as performing as actors. Kunda's study revealed the paradoxical spiral of contribution and opposition to control mechanisms in which the cleverest manipulators can be ultimately unmasked as dupes, and victims show how dignity can be preserved in situations of threat and anxiety. In a similar vein, Leidner showed how McDonald's, programming the manual operations of its employees to the last detail, left their heads free to think what they please. Combined Insurance, unable to control the actual behavior of its agents selling insurance in the field, did not bother to prescribe operations but attempted to indoctrinate their way of thinking. Instead of 'solving' the paradoxes as a naïve realist text would, these books preserve them, revealing paradoxicality and irony as the staple diet of organization members.

Another interesting possibility is *microrealism*, grounded in ethnomethodological approaches (samples can be found in Boden and Zimmerman 1991). If the name were not claimed by another kind of studies, these should be called *naturalist* for their attempt faithfully to portray life in the field. My favorite ergonography of this kind is David Silverman and Jill Jones's *Organizational Work* (1976), which described the minutiae of job recruitment and promotion mechanisms in what appears to be a public administration agency. As through a magnifying glass, we can see in the records of job interviews and similar organizational events just how an organization reproduced itself by carefully selecting 'matching' candidates according to criteria that become clear only after a conversation has taken place. Each interview contributed to the organizational life not only by producing or rejecting a new job recruit but also, and perhaps more importantly, by restating the identity of the organization in question. If we were to follow Van Maanen's (1988) example and look for an analogy in painting, pointillism comes to mind, so detailed is the picture.

A third possibility that comes to mind is a *polyphonic realism*: Latour's study of a project organization, *Aramis or the Love of Technology* (1996), which I discuss in Chapters 6 and 7, is an excellent example of it. A more modest version of the same approach can be found in my own attempt to depict action nets within the Swedish public sector. The doings in and of such an action net can be rendered by an outside observer as a multiplicity of voices coming from different sites and therefore all with their own standpoint (Czarniawska 1997).

The simultaneous presence of contradictory narratives creates a permanent state of paradox. Resolving this paradox, the effort that Luhmann (1991) calls *deparadoxifying*, is the daily work of those Sisyphuses of modern organizations who end their day achieving order and rationality, only to find the paradox back at their door as they come in next morning. Quasi-literary forms help to render the complexity of their experience.

Such complex processes are in a similar vein explored by anthropologists (for a review, see Marcus and Fischer, 1986), ethnomethodologists (e.g. Boden 1994) and sociologists of science and technology (e.g. Ashmore *et al.* 1989), who are also experimenting with polyphonic writings. Law (1994) and Watson (1994) employed ethnographic writing in search of illuminating not only the practices of the field but also the topic of their disciplines—social order in the case of Law and management in the case of Watson.

Ergonography, as a subgenre of organization studies, will thus have narratives as an important (although not the only) material and a crucial (although not sole) device; it will additionally use the insights of literary theory as help in self-reflection. It might facilitate an escape from the inherited image of organization theory as a defective science, which aspires to heights represented by natural sciences without ever quite reaching them. I do not suggest that it should become a defective fiction instead. I argue for a conscious and reflective creation of a specific genre, which recognizes its tradition without being paralyzed by it, which seeks inspiration in other genres without imitating them, and which derives confidence from the importance of its topic and from its own growing skills.

What may be disconcerting is, once more, the postulated closeness between business administration and literary theory. Are ergonographies fiction?

I have already discussed the spuriousness of the difference between 'fact' and 'fiction' in Chapter 3. Additionally, as pointed out by Watts (1990), many works of 'fiction' are based on sound ethnologic studies. As Geertz (1988) observed, the resistance to the notion that ethnographic writing requires the employment of stories, pictures, symbols, and metaphors is due to the confusion between the imagined and the imaginary, the fictive and the false, 'making things out' and 'making them up' (p. 140).

The second expected difference would be that of style. Both types of accounts can, however, be written in the conventional realistic mode, with the use of dialogues to increase credibility. Scientific realism differs from fictional realism in its textual strategy of inviting readers to inspect the source of facts (Latour 1988*b*). In terms of frequency of occurrence, this is correct, although the same strategy has been faked in fiction.

The third difference is a more frequent 'authoring' of fiction works as opposed to the 'writing' of scientific texts. The removal of this difference does not have to lead to tedious self-presentations or to an explicit self-reflection. Even self-explanatory texts use a variety of authorial textual strategies (Eco 1979/1983), of which the impression of 'automatic writing' is perhaps the least attractive.

A role of the organization researcher, as I said before, resides somewhere between a novelist and a literary critic. And it is not the difference between fact and fiction that tells us from the novelists and the critics; it is the kind of texts we analyze and the kind of texts we write.

Practitioners and consultants are busy writing texts and authoring works. The researchers' role is to interpret these texts (although it requires creation of yet another text). They build worlds; we inspect the construction (although it requires a construction of yet another world).

This is, in fact, a double task. First we must give room to a conventional narrative, which plays an important role in organizations. But this does not mean a mechanical repetition of it. I may add that even conversation analysts delude themselves as to 'the completeness' of their transcripts. What about body language, smells, and all the other elements of a conversation? Every transcript is an editorial work, and all editorial work should be done with the reader in mind. There are many types of narrative possible in a scientific report. The *dialectical narrative*, for instance, refuses the common-sense notion of a past separate from the present (a past exists only as the present of the narrator, and is needed only to perform shifting operations) and rejects the notion of mechanical causality (*past hoc, ergo propter hoc*) typical of the simple narrative (Lejeune 1989).

The dialectical narrative is only one possible device, perhaps inaccessible to us humble ergonographers. But there are many others: the *dialogical narrative* in the sense proposed by Bakhtin (1981—a text that interrogates the world) or the *interruptive narrative* in the sense proposed by Silverman and Torode (1980—a world that interrogates a text, or maybe just a text that interrogates another text). Taking the risk of imposing a non-existent homogeneity on a variety of approaches and their proponents—dialectical, dialogical, interruptive—I would like to point out two traits that to my mind they have in common. On the one hand, they all set out to preserve the 'straight' narrative of the field. On the other hand, they all claim the right to problematize and to ironize, and this requires an examination of one's own text as well, a self-reflection. Here again we are touching upon the questions of polyphony and representation, which are the topic of Chapter 7.

Before we arrive there, however, let us undertake some more focused excursions into the literary theory and practice, now that their usefulness to management theory and practice seems established. The next chapter takes up the crucial element of the narrative—that is, plot, while the chapter after continues along the same trail by visiting the genre famous for its plots—the detective story.

5

On the Absence of Plot in Organization Studies

On Monday, the Chief Executive Officer (CEO) of a big transnational came to work only after lunch, something that had never happened before. On Tuesday, he disconnected all the telephones and was seen sitting in his office reading Dilbert books. On Wednesday of the same week his secretary opened the door, certain that the office was empty, and discovered the CEO standing on his head against the wall. On Thursday, the CEO came to the office with a group of young people carrying musical instruments. They spent all day in his office. Loud music was heard. On Friday, the CEO asked his secretary to provide him with the most popular women's magazines and went home immediately afterwards.

This is a story without a plot. It is a story, because it reports a chronological sequence of events and actions, it has a main character and some peripheral ones, and even fulfills the classical requirement of the unity of time and place. Still, there is no meaningful connection between the events, apart from sheer chronology. There are some elements of suspense[1] (the CEO's actions seem to deviate from his regular habits), but they are not woven together into any kind of intrigue. The story does not make sense.

On Friday evening the CEO sat at home, thoughtlessly leafing through the magazines. His face went into sudden convulsions and deep cracks showed in his skin. Soon the whole structure of his face collapsed and the emerging head of an Alien became clearly visible . . .

This is perhaps not a strictly organizational story any longer, but it has a plot. The events fall into place, woven together by the last paragraph. Another variation may look as follows:

An earlier version of this chapter was presented at the Scancor Conference 'Samples of the Future', Stanford, 20–22 September, 1998. I thank Bengt Jacobsson and Guje Sevón for comments.

[1] Todorov (1977) would call it 'curiosity' (revealing effects but withholding causes). 'Suspense', according to him, is to reveal causes and withhold the effects. This division coincides with the conventional division of labour between science and literature.

The following Monday, the CEO called all the top managers to his office. 'Well, you all look expectant and with every right. We are going to do a complete overhaul of this company. We will change everything—culture, thinking habits, and furniture. We begin now.'

My contention is that many organization studies reporting fieldwork, that is, trying to re-present organizational practice, resemble the first story. They are systematically presented, usually according to the principle of chronology, they contain a set of characters, have more or less unitary place and time, but contain no plot. As Kenneth Burke (1945/1969) might have said, they have scene and act, agents and agency, but no purpose—and it is the pentad that permits creating a plot.

It is usual to criticize such texts as 'too empirical' or 'atheoretical', but I think that this is not a correct diagnosis. After all, a theory, like a coat, must hang on something—a hook, a hanger, or a body frame. There must first be something to theorize about, and the fact that Tuesday comes after Monday has already received a convincing theoretical explanation. It is not unusual that, in doctoral dissertations, after such an 'empirical' part comes a 'theoretical' one, loosely connected by a kind of common theme. In this case, it could be 'middle age crisis', 'leadership', or anything else. It is only the second ending, however, that calls specifically for theories of leadership or organizational change. The first ending calls for a theory of Alien invasion.

Even if we assume that good stories do have a plot, why should organization studies contain stories at all? And if they should, why are these stories plotless?

As to the first question, I have attempted to answer it in earlier chapters (and also in Czarniawska 1997, 1998), so I shall only briefly recapitulate my argument. The narrative has always played an important part in the production and distribution of human knowledge. Although not a trademark of scientific texts, the narrative is always present. It plays an even more prominent part in organizational practice, which is yet another reason to treat it with care. And to treat it with care means to construct and to develop it well, learning from those whose speciality it is.

As to the second question—that is, the reasons for the absence of plot in organization studies—the answers to this will have to wait until the notion of plot is better introduced.

THE PLOT

Although the notion of plot (*mythos*) takes an important place in Aristotle's *Poetics*, it is a commonplace expression in literary theory, which means that it is often used but rarely defined. Suffice it to say that there exists a whole book dedicated to plot (Dipple 1970), which talks about the plot but not what it is. The author does repeat, after Aristotle, that 'plot is the arrangement of action' (p. 43) but action can also be arranged alphabetically in a text. Elisabeth

Dipple, however, quotes an essay on 'The Structure of the Novel' by Edwin Muir (1928), who is more specific in saying that 'the term plot . . . designates . . . the chain of events in a story and the principle which knits it together' (after Dipple 1970: 25). Forster in his essay 'Aspects of the Novel' (1927) developed the Aristotelian distinction between a simple story ('a narrative of events arranged in their time-sequence') and a plot that arranges them according to a sense of causality (after *Encyclopaedia Britannica* 1989; Micropaedia, ix. 523).

The Russian Formalists went further in emphasizing the difference between *fabula* (the story) and *sujet* (the plot) but, in contrast to Aristotle, they accentuated the artifice of the plot, as opposed to the 'naturalness' of the story (White 1973; Todorov 1977; Selden 1985). A more relevant way of conceiving of this difference is that of Bakhtin/Medvedev (1928/1994), who stressed the plot's focus on the relation between the narrator and the audience, rather than between the text and the world.

Donald Polkinghorne (1987), attempting to narrow the gap between psychology and narrative knowledge, dedicated much attention to the role of the plot and its possible uses in the human sciences: 'The plot functions to transform a chronicle or listing of events into a schematic whole by highlighting and recognizing the contribution that certain events make to the development of the whole' (pp. 18–19). But not only that: a plot can weave into the story the historical and social context, information about physical laws and thoughts and feelings reported by people. 'A plot has the capacity to articulate and consolidate complex threads of multiple activities by means of the overlay of subplots' (p. 19). This is an important property from the point of view of organization students, faced often with the fact that, as many things happen simultaneously, a simple chronology is not sufficient to tell a case story. And this analogy is not accidental: 'The recognition or construction of a plot employs the kind of reasoning that Charles Peirce called "abduction", the process of suggesting a hypothesis that can serve to explain some puzzling phenomenon. Abduction produces a conjecture that is tested by fitting it over the "facts" ' (p. 19). Lastly but most importantly, 'more than one plot can provide a meaningful constellation and integration for the same set of events, and different plot organizations change the meaning of the individual events as their roles are reinterpreted according to their functions in different plots' (p. 19). A lavish office party has a different meaning in the story of a success than in the story of a bankruptcy.

The most quoted example of a basic plot is that by Todorov (1990), who, although perceived as a successor of the Formalists, declares himself as navigating away from both 'impressionist writing' and 'terroristic formalism'. His definition, or rather description, says that

The minimal complete plot consists in the passage from one equilibrium to another. An 'ideal' narrative begins with a stable situation which is disturbed by some power or force. There results a state of disequilibrium; by the action or a force directed in the opposite direction, the equilibrium is re-established; the second equilibrium is similar to the first, but the two are never identical.   (Todorov 1977: 11).

This 'minimal' plot is also what Propp (1968) called a 'move', and most tales contain more than one move, which must be connected to one another. Such a combination of plots is usually achieved, says Todorov (1977), by one of two strategies: *linking* (coordination)—i.e. adding simple plots to one another so they fit—and *embedding* (subordination)—i.e. setting one plot inside the other. One can add, after White (1973), that, like a historian, an organization student confronts 'a veritable chaos of events *already constituted*, out of which he must choose the elements of the story he would tell' (p. 6 n. 5). Thus a necessity of two additional tactics: *exclusion* and *emphasis* (also, embedding can serve both combination and selection).

From what has been said before, it can be concluded that the difference between a plotless and a plotted story is that the first hangs on sheer chronology, whereas the second relies on causality (including intentionality). A poor storyteller hopes that chronology will stand for causality; a clever storyteller sells chronology for causality (what happens earlier causes what happens next (see Bruner 1990)). But even a clever storyteller could not make chronology pass for causality in the story I concocted in the beginning. This is because the elements of this story are connected by *succession* only; to become a fully plotted story, they need also to be related by *transformation* (Todorov 1990). This is achieved only by adding the last paragraph, by which strange consequent events (that is, the two first elements of a plot, an—assumed—'normal state' and repeated deviations) become a new state of affairs (an invasion of a body snatcher, a renewal campaign). A plotted story thus involves not only a *syntagmatic* dimension (and and and) but also a *paradigmatic* one (see Chapter 3).

ALL PLOT, NO STORY OR ALL STORY, NO PLOT?

Before I embark on an attempt to read organizational texts (and some non-organizational ones as well) with what is clearly a set of structuralist devices, I need to make a caveat. My attempt is made in a post-structuralist spirit; that is, I am fully aware that I am placing the structures onto the texts rather than finding them there, and that my attempt in itself is nothing but a plot construction, which can be evaluated by the readers in the same manner.

I shall start with James G. March and Herbert A. Simon's *Organizations* (1958/1993) as an exemplar of elegant organizational writing that contains a plot but no story. Plot, in this context, means the structure based on causality rather than sequentiality, on transformation rather than succession.

According to the authors themselves, the purpose behind the book was to make a 'propositional inventory' of theory about organizations. 'Of course, to inventory propositions one has to organize them, and so the book that evolved from this exercise also proposed a structure of organization theory' (March and Simon, 1958/1993: 1).

This comment itself should be an important lesson for aspiring writers in organization theory. Fieldwork, or literature studies, always result in a pile of entities: propositions, categories, events, actions, numbers. They have to be connected—that is, organized. Grounded theory, for example, suggested an 'organic' way of making connections, so that the pile never rose above the author's head: a new category had to be fitted immediately to the categories already existing before a search for further categories could continue (Glaser and Strauss 1967).

Despite the common-sense wisdom that grounded theory offered us all, we continue first to pile, and then to sort, and then to connect. Sorting and connecting can be the same operation (again, embedding is a good example— two narratives are separated as subordinated to one another), or they can proceed in an opposite direction—sorting severs connection, which then must be re-established again. This can be done on a mechanical basis; for example, in alphabetical order, in order of magnitude, or in chronological order. As I said before, a chronological order may pass for a meaningful order when chronology is taken for causality. Causality is, however, the usual connecting ideal of scientific writing.[2]

The plot of *Organizations* can be summarized as follows. In Western societies systems of coordinated action called formal organizations exist whose survival depends on transforming conflict into cooperation, mobilization of resources, and coordination of efforts. These three are accomplished mainly through 'control over information, identities, stories and incentives' (March and Simon 1958/1993: 2) but imperilled by 'the uncertainties and ambiguities of life, by the limited cognitive and affective capabilities of human actors, by the complexities . . . and by threats . . .' (ibid.). Organizational actors cope with these limitations 'by calculations, planning, and analysis, by learning from their experience and knowledge of others, and by creating and using systems of rules, procedures, and interpretations that store understanding in easily retrievable form. They weave supportive cultures, agreements, structures, and beliefs around their activities' (ibid.).

The causal structure is very clear. Organizations survive because/when they are able satisfactorily to fulfil the three conditions guaranteeing survival. There are obstacles on the way to achieving those conditions and these are tackled within a variety of coping mechanisms, which become stabilized to facilitate the coping.

This plot, however, can never be applied to a story, for at least two reasons. One is supplied by the authors themselves. In the hindsight of the thirty-five years since the book was first published, 'the greatest deficiency in the book is its treatment of empirical evidence' (March and Simon 1958/1993: 5). The first five chapters deal with the history of organization theory and then with matters of motivation, etc., where psychological studies, mostly of experimental character,

---

[2]   I apologize to all phenomenologists for a ruthless treatment of intentionality as a kind of causality in this text. Although philosophically it is much more complicated, these two are equivalent as text-structuring devices.

are quoted. Chapters 6 and 7 deal with organizations—that is, systems and not individuals—and here experiments are difficult to perform. The authors explain that

Most of the relevant evidence we found took the form of monographic studies of particular organizations—case studies—and there was nothing in the extant literature on scientific methodology that told us how to make case studies into the sort of objective, reproducible, representative evidence that we were taught science is founded on. (ibid.)

In such a forensic model of science, stories are not accepted as evidence. As in a police investigation, a story may lead to a discovery of a proof, but in itself will never be accepted as evidence. Also, as Polkinghorne pointed out, within the logico-scientific mode of knowing, an explanation is achieved by recognizing an event as an instance of a general law, or as belonging to a certain category. Not so in the narrative mode of knowing:

When a human event is said not to make sense, it is usually not because a person is unable to place it into the proper category. The difficulty stems, instead, from a person's inability to integrate the event into a plot whereby it becomes understandable in the context of what has happened . . . Thus, narratives exhibit explanation instead of demonstrating it.   (Polkinghorne 1987: 21)

   In order to be used as evidence, stories would have to be collected systematically and transformed into 'data'. At the time March and Simon's book was first written, people who studied organizing in its actual context were 'operating largely in the mode of social historians or ethnographers. Their samples were samples of opportunity, representing no definable universe. Their data consisted largely of historical narratives, the causal connections induced by a liberal application of common sense and organizational shrewdness' (March and Simon, 1958/1993: 6). In the intervening thirty-five years, though, many more studies of that kind were conducted. 'The increasing attention being paid by social scientists today to the work of social historians and ethnographers is a good omen of greater willingness to take case studies and historical narratives seriously as data for discovering and testing theories of organization' (ibid.). When, however, such transformation is achieved, they will not be stories anymore, and thus my idea of a 'story with a plot' will not be actualized.

   What if, assuming a great tolerance of the famous authors, one should attempt a reverse operation, using their model as a plot in a story? I do not think this is possible, either, the reason being that, while plots in stories are linear, or at best spiral, this plot is circular. It is not static: things happen, obstacles arise and are coped with, but there is no state of equilibrium to return to, or even a clear state of disequilibrium. Until organizations die, they operate as a kind of a *perpetuum mobile*. Coordination, mobilization, and transformation of conflicts into a cooperation continue in the face of limited rationality of people, ambiguity of life, and complexity of the world.

   Philip Selznick's *TVA and the Grass Roots* (1949) is an example not so much of 'all story no plot' but rather of 'a story and a plot', which is perhaps the most typical case in organization studies.

I acquired my copy of Selznick's book second-hand. It carried the traces of its previous owner(s): marks, comments, annotations etc. Most of these were contained in Part One: Official Doctrine and in Conclusions. There were some comments in chapters V and VI of Part Two, and in chapter VII of Part Three, but only at the beginning of the chapters. Chapters III and IV, which carry the main bulk of the story, were untouched. I thought at first that this was just a typical example of student reading: the beginning to get the gist of it, the end to see what is important, and some checks in the middle just to see whether anything important has been missed. As my repeated readings (I use Selznick both in my teaching and in my writing) conformed to the same pattern, however, I began to suspect that there was more to it than just a lazy reader. It would be impossible, for example, to read Veblen (1899/1994) in this way, although some of his stories may seem tedious or alien to a contemporary reader.

Selznick's book has an excellent plot, which can be simplified along Todorov's outline. An ideology (the grass-roots doctrine) gives rise to a large collective enterprise. Alas, the unanticipated consequences of organized action pose obstacles to the fulfillment of the doctrine. The organization formed in the course of the enterprise combats these obstacles by co-optation, contributing to its own survival and the popularity, although not necessarily the realization, of the doctrine.

This is a powerful and an important plot, recently reformulated by Latour in his 'Power of Associations' (1986). Studying 'power structures', he says, not only solidifies these structures but also mystifies their origins. People and organizations that appear powerful do so because they successfully hide a fragile network of associations behind them and the (seldom glorious) history of their construction. The researchers should be inspecting (or retrospecting) the work in progress, not admiring (or despairing over) the result.

What Selznick did, however, was to pack his plot with illustrations from the story itself into Part One and Conclusions, sprinkling some of it into the first pages of chapters V, VI, and VII. All metaphors and the logic of the action are laid bare there. The rest contains the story (actually, several of them) and the facts. Chapters III and IV are the most telling in so far as they share the same title: III. TVA and the Farm Leadership: The Construction of an Administrative Constituency; IV. TVA and the Farm Leadership (Continued). Most likely, the publisher told Selznick that a chapter of seventy pages would not do, so it got divided into two parts. What a disarming way of admitting that there is no internal structure that would permit a meaningful division of the chapter. When sheer chronology is the connecting device, a separation may occur at any point. 'It's getting late, I will tell you the rest tomorrow.'

What Selznick did amounts to telling the readers: here is the plot, and here is the story, now apply one to the other. Imagine a detective story that says at the outset who was killed, by whom, how and why, and then relates, hour after hour, all that was said and done during a certain period of time. Such a deconstructive experiment might have been done, but once only, just to reveal the implausibility of it and the need for plotting.

And yet in organization studies this experiment is repeated over and over again. There is, of course, an abyss of difference between the skill of Selznick and that of desperate doctoral students concocting 'an empirical' and 'a theoretical' part of their dissertations, but the idea is the same.

Might it not be a trademark, a characteristic, that distinguishes organization studies as a genre from detective stories and all other genres? It might, but perhaps it is a difference worth thinking over. There is no fatalism in any genre development. Alternative institutionalization processes are always possible.

In the late 1920s, after a quick and spectacular success, the genre of detective stories seemed to be falling into disrepute. A Detection Club of England was founded in 1928, and settled upon the work of systematizing the props of the genre with the purpose of outlawing the most exploited and improbable plots, caricature-like characters, and other outrages that had emerged (Melling 1996). This attempt at policing led to some intended and many unintended consequences. Ronald A. Knox in England and S. S. Van Dine in the USA made lists of rules to be followed by serious crime writers (Melling 1996).

What was feared was the impoverishment of a genre stifled by rules too clearly drawn.[3] The result was the opposite. The standardizing attempts gave rise, on the one hand, to countless attempts at reproduction. Symons (1972/1992) says that the number of detective stories reviewed by the US *Book Review Digest* grew from 12 in 1914 to 217 in 1939, and, although reviews may have stabilized since, publications continue to grow at the same pace. On the other hand, the standards formed an excellent basis for all kinds of parody, pastiche, and creative transformations. The two forces combined resulted in the detective story living through a golden age again, much as in the 1930s. Any attempt at renewal requires a clear formulation of a tradition against which to rebel (Alexandersson and Trossmark 1997). Before I turn to what can be considered an alternative type of canon in organization studies, I shall make an excursion into a well-plotted terrain: that of fiction and of the sociology of science and technology.

THE WELL-PLOTTED STORY

I will now examine two stories enriched by a plot—one classified by the bookstore personnel as 'fiction', the other as 'social science', although, as the quotation marks suggest, the difference is rather spurious. These stories not only

---

[3]   Similar expressions of fear greeted Pfeffer's (1993) appeal to solidify the genre of organization studies (which he calls a paradigm). The (negative) reactions to his appeal already exhibit a dynamics similar to that described above (see Burrell *et al.* 1994; Perrow 1994; Van Maanen 1995*a,b*).

join sequentiality and causality/intentionality, succession and transformation, but also bridge the division instituted by the Formalists, telling a story and being aware of creating it in the narration. Plot and story, *sujet* and *fabula*, are one text.

I have chosen William Boyd's *Armadillo* (1998), because it contains a solid portion of organization theory, and also because Boyd is one of the leading writers of my generation. *Armadillo* has two interlinked but parallel plots, only one of which is an 'organization story' and will be focused on here. The main character, Lorrimer Black, comes from an immigrant family (a fact that he hides behind his taken name) and makes a comet-like career as a loss adjuster in a big British company, Fortress Sure. The suicide of an owner of a burnt factory who had claimed insurance sets off a series of events that put a stop to Black's career.

Lorrimer perceives his job as problem- and puzzle-solving—that is, decision-making, and a supporting flow of activities consisting in relating to his colleagues and his bosses. He is good at both. All of a sudden, however, both turn out to be impossible tasks, surpassing the capacity of all standard procedures that Lorrimer developed with great care. He finds himself not in an organizational but an interorganizational quandary. This is further complicated by the fact that loss adjustment is a peculiar profession, that of an investigator and of an auditor, a finance person and a psychologist. Lorrimer is a natural talent, and one of his bosses calls him 'a brilliant young samurai', no doubt in preparation for what happens next. Black gets fired, because he is the weakest link in the network, and because he actually manages to figure out the complicated pattern of events and interlocking interests, although, in unison with other postmodern detectives (see Chapter 6), he realizes that 'the truth' is unreachable: 'He wondered if he would ever discover what had really been at stake in the Fedora Palace affair, what the true rewards were for the participants. He strongly doubted it' (p. 285). What is clear is that he was made into a scapegoat, and his bosses openly admitted it, making vague promises to repay him in the future. Lorrimer denounces them, and embarks on a new life together with the woman of his dreams. The last time the readers meet him, however, is in the airport lounge, his flight immediately departing, waiting for the woman who might or might not come. The reader will never know whether Lorrimer is facing a brilliant future, or a way back to his apartment, unemployed, his life threatened by people whom he exposed. One thing is clear: this is not a story about how virtue becomes rewarded in the end.

Thanks to the continuous tension of the plot the readers, propelled by their curiosity, are forced to learn quite a lot about organizing, and especially about the business of insurance. *Armadillo* contains a well-developed organization theory, which can, in fact, be seen as a third plot. To begin with, it shows how illusive is the fiction of 'organization' as a closed group of people, a quasi-culture, a quasi-family, living their common fate on the same premises. Although the employees of Fortress Sure, like all other organizational members, try to enact this fiction, cultivating formal and informal hierarchies, developing quasi-personal relationships, etc., the very nature of their jobs shatters this illusion. Fortress Sure is but a small and tentative node in several networks that are huge and overpower not only individuals, but organizations as well. Black's contacts with the upper echelons of the hierarchy reveal the Fortress's entrenchment in the British class structure with its nepotism and power games. Lorrimer's job as a loss adjuster forces him daily into the life of other organizations—building constructors, hotel owners, investors, show business—not allowing him to keep within the safe boundaries of Fortress Sure.

But the most important of those networks, at least for Lorrimer but perhaps for contemporary societies in general, is the profession. Insurance, with its norms, values, and best practices, is strongly controlling the actions of both Lorrimer and his boss, who was his mentor before he became his enemy. Lorrimer is not a virtuous individual facing a monstrous organization or a group of villainous people; he is a conscientious professional who accidentally gets trapped in the requirements of his own profession.

The readers receive not only a brief history of insurance, but its philosophical basis as well:

What does insurance do, really do? Hogg [Lorrimer's superior] would ask us. And we would say, diligently echoing the textbooks, that insurance's primary function is to substitute certainty for uncertainty as regards the economic consequences of disastrous events. It gives a sense of security in an insecure world. It makes you feel safe, then? Hogg would follow up. Yes, we would reply: something tragic, catastrophic, troublesome or irritating may have occurred but there is a recompense in the form of a preordained sum of money. All is not entirely lost . . .

That attitude, Hogg would say, is fundamentally immoral. Immoral, dishonest and misleading. Such an understanding promotes and bolsters the fond notion that we will all grow up, be happy, healthy, find a job, fall in love, start a family, earn a living, retire, enjoy a ripe old age and die peacefully in our sleep. This is a seductive dream, Hogg would snarl, the most dangerous fantasy. All of us know that, in reality, life never works out like this. So what did we do? We invented insurance—which makes us feel we have half a chance, a shot at achieving it, so that even if something goes wrong . . . we have provided some buffer against random disaster.

But, Hogg would say, why should a system that we have invented not possess the same properties as the life we lead? Why should insurance be solid and secure? What right do we have to think that the laws of uncertainty which govern the human condition, all human endeavour, all human life, do not apply to this artificial construct . . .? (Boyd 1998: 12–43).

This lengthy quote is inserted here to illustrate several points at once. The moral of Boyd's book is that ambiguity is the human condition, the starting and ending point, and not a temporary deviation from the ordered state of things (Boyd thus radicalizes the garbage-can model, see below). People sometimes try to enhance the state of ambiguity, as when trying to change their lives and to start a new business, and sometimes to reduce it by repeating, by ordering, by regulating, and by institutionalizing. This ought to be a starting point of all organization theory, so that 'intended consequences' may become its main puzzle, and not the other way around.[4]

In the book, nothing ends as planned: not the insurance fraud, not the bosses' attempt to cover it up, and not Lorrimer's way out. Because, as Hogg says, why should insurance be sure? And here is another lesson for organizational theory and practice: all attempts focused on reducing ambiguity and uncertainty must, per definition, be as ambiguity ridden as everything else. We may, like the institutionalist theorists, metaphorically travel outside the system in order to have a look at it, but even such a symbolic excursion has all the properties of the system it tries to capture from the outside. 'The outside' is a figment of our imagination, albeit a very useful one.

Last but not least I would like to attract attention to the style of the quote. If one took away the stylistic insertions indicating that a dialogue takes place ('Hogg would say'), we would have a text not very different from a social-science theory. Even with the dialogue, Hogg is just using the Socratic method of teaching. From that unapologetic loan one can also deduce that, unlike organization scholars, literary people rarely ask the question: 'But is *this* a novel?' but rather: 'Is it interesting? Is it beautiful? Does it work?'

Not that attempts at crossing genre boundaries are completely unknown in the social sciences. I will now turn to one that I consider particularly instructive.

Aramis or the Love of Technology (Latour 1996) is a story of an automated train system that was tried in Paris and then abandoned. It begins, innocently enough, as a combination of two classic plots, one a detective story—who killed Aramis?—and the other a *Bildungsroman*, a story of a pupil learning from the master. The first plot depends for its pull on curiosity: the readers know the effects, Aramis is dead and buried in the Museum of Technology, and the cause is looked for—who did it? The second plot, embedded in the first, depends on the push of (mild) suspense: given the Pupil's hunger for knowledge and the Master's abundance of it, the readers might fairly surely expect an enlightened Pupil in the end, but they may count on various complications in his way.

Complications, when they arrive, are not of the manageable kind, which are the stuff of fairy tales. The obstacles stand in the way, not so much of the heroes, but of the plots. The main plot, that of detecting those guilty of killing an innovation, proves to be unfeasible. At a certain point there are twenty contradictory interpretations offered for the demise of the Aramis project (Latour himself counts them elsewhere), all of them correct. Just before the final report has to be produced, the Master (and not the Pupil, as he should) vanishes, not because the Pupil has to learn autonomy, but because the Master has more important things to think about.

---

[4]   Michael Burawoy (1979) made a similar reversal when he decided that the standard question 'Why don't workers work harder' should, in the face of organizational reality, be replaced by 'Why do workers work so hard?'.

What was a detective story turns into a tragic love story. Aramis has not been killed; it is just that nobody loved him enough to keep him alive. His less attractive rival, the metro system VAL, is loved and lives happily in Lille; a new Aramis is being born in San Diego—will it live?

The *Bildungsroman* turns into its opposite, a tormented inner journey of the Master into self-reflection, doubt, and fear. The Pupil gets his grade and tries to ignore the ramblings of his former Master, whose excessive reflection makes him turn against the sacred values of the society, and *contrast* research with science:

'Oh, you do love science! You were formed by it in your graduate schools. As for technology, you drank in its certainties with your mother's milk. But you still don't love research. Its uncertainties, its whirlwinds, its mixed characters, its setbacks, its negotiations, its compromises—you turn all that over to politicians, journalists, union leaders, sociologists, writers, and literary critics; to me, and people like me. Research, for you, is the tub of the Danaïdes: it's discussion leading nowhere, it's a dancer in a tutu, it's democracy. But technological research is the exact opposite of science, the exact opposite of technology.' Latour 1996: 293).

Harsh words in the context of organization research that often aspires to a technology-like status. Is management research the opposite of management? I believe it is, but it is a difficult message to convey, so that even Master delivers it in a final outburst of anger and pain, hardly a conventional ending for an organization study.

Even worse, the device of changing horses in midstream—that is, transforming the main plots of the story—is a tricky business. One danger is obvious: the author might drown. Aramis, Master, and their author survive the journey very well, but it does take a masterly driver.

Another danger is with the readers: they may not like the play of plots. Bronwyn Davies (1989) read feminist fairy tales to pre-school children, where plot was intact but the functions of characters were reversed. It was the princess, for example, who saved the silly, pretty prince from the dragon and then left him. Davies's small listeners did interpretive wonders in order to save the proper plot: as a result of her efforts the princess became dirty and poor and therefore understood herself, they explained, not to be a proper wife for the prince . . . Readers might resort to murder in order to save 'their' plots, at least symbolically.

Latour saved himself by doing a revolutionary transformation of plots but ended up with another set of recognizable and legitimate plots. Herein lies another complication in transferring his kind of experiment to organization studies. It assumes a reader well familiar with all the variety of plots in both fiction and sociology. While organization scholars are no doubt as well versed in fiction as anybody else, they are less used to a reflection over their own genre (the genre as a result being less defined), and such clever tricks may well be lost in the void. I believe that organization studies must look for exemplars within its own genre, and then develop it, both from within and by excursions to and loans from other genres. The present repertoire of plots may be rather meager:

there is an internal problem in a company and it must be solved; a company loses its shares in the market; a new technology is found; a new competitor emerges. This is the first step, the disequilibrium. The next step proceeds along the well-known logic of rationality (the strongest plot so far) and ends up either with the equilibrium restored, or with the conclusion that there are unintended consequences. What could be of help to many writers aspiring to go beyond this kind of plot in organization stories is a *protoplot*, or a set of basic elements enabling a construction of all kinds of interesting plots. My suggestion is that the garbage-can model can serve as such a protoplot.

THE GARBAGE-CAN MODEL AS A PROTOPLOT

There is general agreement that the garbage can is a model of decision-making in organizations. The problem is, however, that, for instance, *Webster's New Collegiate Dictionary* (1981: 732) lists twelve different meanings of the word 'model'. Sifting out the most obviously inappropriate ones, there are still quite a few possibilities left:

4: a miniature representation of something; *also*: a pattern of something to be made 5: an example for imitation or emulation . . . 7: ARCHETYPE . . . 11: a description or an analogy used to help visualize something (as an atom) that cannot be directly observed.

The meanings numbered 5 and 11 seem to be most relevant: surely the authors intended their model as an analogy (or rather a metaphor) to help visualize the hidden intricacies of decision-making and, had they succeeded, the emulation would follow? I would like to argue that, precisely if they had succeeded, the emulation would not follow. For, if an illuminating metaphor has been coined or a useful analogy found, nothing can be done with it by subsequent researchers but a critique or eventual replacement. Certainly, a successful model has a great educational value—after all, teaching is the biggest market for models. In terms of further construction of meaning, however—i.e. sense-making rather than sense-giving (Weick 1995), the more attractive the model the smaller its heuristic value. Good old positivists knew what they were doing when, before engaging in any intellectual enterprise of their own, they mercilessly ground the theories of their predecessors until they revealed a flaw, a gap, a sign of cracking. A perfect model can only be reused, and the added meaning value diminishes with every use. This is why the dream of an 'accumulating body of knowledge' has never been fulfilled. It would surely be possible to 'apply' the garbage-can model to all kinds of organizations and then repeat the enterprise to add the time dimension, but that would wear out the model to a thin platitude rather than making it universally valid.

What, then, if we turn back to the other two meanings of the word 'model', those numbered 4 and 7? I shall try to argue that the garbage-can model can be seen as a pattern of something to be made—certainly not for decisions in organizations, but for *studies* of organizing—and this because it contains, or consists of, a complete set of elements for the basic unit of social life—a drama. Let me quote from Kenneth Burke (with apologies for the chauvinist-naturalist vocabulary of his times):

What is involved, when we say what people are doing and why they are doing it? . . . the basic forms of thought which, in accordance with the nature of the world as all men necessarily experience it, are exemplified in attributing of motives. These forms of thought . . . are equally present in systematically elaborated metaphysical structures, in legal judgments, in poetry and fiction, in political and scientific works, in news and in bits of gossip offered at random.   (Burke 1945/1969: p. xv).

Although the authors of the garbage-can model do not mention Burke as their forefather (see Cohen *et al.* 1972/1988: 296 n. 2), the models are in perfect synchrony, which can be explained by the fact that they both capture the archetype of human action.[5] If I may be permitted to mix the two vocabularies, are not decisions what was done (Act), choice opportunities when and where it was done (Scene), participants those who did it (Agents), problems why they did it (Purpose), and solutions the means (Agency)? At any given time/place, there is an accessible (wider) and legitimate (narrower) repertoire of all the five elements, and rules of appropriateness that say how to connect them (more about those later).

A certain difficulty arises at this point. Hopefully, I have shown the parallel between the two models coming from two different disciplines; I might even have succeeded in translating them into one another. But this still leaves us with the meaning of the word 'model' as in number 11: now we have a double description of a certain process, and all it may cause is an *embarras de richesse*: why two models when one is enough? I can hear Ockham sharpening his razor.

The reason I translated a model from organization theory into literary theory is to show that it can be used in the same way as in literary theory: as help in constructing a plot. As a *protoplot*, it guarantees a reliable and attractive pattern of what is to be built. At the same time, it leaves all the glory to the constructor, in whose hands lie the plotting work. Now, then, it is time to ask how the five elements may be connected? There are some answers concerning this in both the dramatist pentad and in the garbage-can model.

CONSTRUCTING THE PLOT

Burke is all prepared to give advice to the potential plotter, albeit on a general level. A successful drama (that is, convincing, gripping, credible, beautiful, or

---

5   I leave aside the issue whether archetypes are, as Jung and after him Frye (1957/1990) believed, expressions of deep and universal human nature or, as Steiner (1975/1992) claims, acute observations already made by the ancient Greeks which we since then translate into still newer versions.

all of these) is characterized by a consistency in the pentad. The five elements must be consistent with one another. A breach of such consistency, although it can also be used for plotting purposes, is immediately discovered by the public. If a scene portrays an *agora*, we do not expect Roman gladiators to enter it and commence a fight. Similarly, if a scene represented a colosseum, we would be disconcerted to witness Greek citizens conducting a debate there. Some additional steps must be taken to explain the inconsistency, as in Woody Allen's movie *Mighty Aphrodite* where a Greek chorus sings Broadway songs on a Roman arena (the explanation restoring consistency in this case is Woody Allen himself).

This observation seems plausible both to common sense and to narratologists, and is supported by many who embrace the coherence principle (an example from social sciences is Fisher 1984, 1987). There is but one question to ask: who decides what is consistent and what is not and by what criteria? If we do not answer this question, we just explain *ignotum per ignotum*, or rather replace one unexplained word with another: 'convincing' with 'consistent', or 'credible' with 'coherent'.

Here Burke could use some help from the authors of the garbage-can model, although from another work of theirs (March and Olsen 1989). Scene and act ratio is perceived as coherent when it conforms to the appropriate (legitimate for a given time and place) rules of coherence. Or, as Mary Douglas (1986) briskly says, sameness is decided by institutions. Plots, like everything else, are ruled by the rules of appropriateness. Being a pragmatist, I would go even further and claim that there are no such rules: there is a repertoire of plots, which is recognizable by a certain time/place collective, and within that subrepertoires, which are perceived as appropriate for connecting certain types of scenes, agents, acts, purposes, and agencies. The actual plot construction consists of either reproduction, paraphrase, or rebellion against those.[6] In the example at the beginning of this chapter, the second plot is an appropriate one. The first plot attempts a rebellion, but observe that it simply substitutes one convention for another. The inappropriate plot is still taken from the same repertoire and therefore it can be recognized and thought amusing/outrageous/silly but still understandable.

Now, back to the garbage-can model. It was not designed like the dramatist pentad, and therefore it can be suspected of having its own hints as to possible emplotments. My reading is that it introduces a powerful element of the Scene that was well known to the ancient Greeks but is almost forgotten by the contemporary organization theorists: Chance. It is by chance that certain ingredients fall into the same garbage can at the same time. Here, however, the Greeks had one advantage: for them, Chance was but a servant of fate, and Fate was the ultimate plotter. By what process, however, do the four random

---

[6]   The very process of revealing a belongingness of a plot to a distinct genre is in itself constitutive of meaning. White (1973) called it *explanation by emplotment* and Kaj Sköldberg (1994) uses it in organization theory.

ingredients produce the fifth, that is, the act, or the decision? Surely not with the help of the laws of gravity and chemical decomposition.

This is, of course, not a critique of the garbage-can model. Like every power-ful metaphor, it acquires its force by bridging things and events that were never before thought to be alike. It is when forced to act as analogies that metaphors break down. Another example at hand is that of isomorphism: the metaphor is so powerful that it is taken on unreflectively. Which is, however, if any, the anal-ogy between the physical and the chemical properties of crystals and of human organizations? *How* does isomorphism happen between organiza-tions?

Bernward Joerges and I suggested once, half-playfully, a possible answer to this question: 'our stance is one of the same level as organizational actors: we sit inside, or in any event within listening range of the garbage can, in order to follow how the actors try to put together ideas and actions to come to them, in their never ending activity of sense-making' (Czarniawska and Joerges 1995: 173). In a similar vein Ellen S. O'Connor, who also noticed garbage-can narra-tive potential, said that 'each individual participant in the decision and action process contributes strands to the larger tapestry of the decision–action scenario' (1997: 396)

With this addition, the garbage-can model can serve as a protoplot, like the dramatist pentad, for construction of organization studies. Plotting itself can be done either by organizational actors (that is, selected by the researcher from various kinds of sensemaking taking place in organizations anyway (see Weick 1995)), or by organization students. The general principle is still Todorov's: a disequilibrium has arisen in one of the three elements: choice opportunities (scene), purpose (problems), agency (solutions). Participants/agents act/decide, thus re-establishing a new equilibrium. Whoever the plotter was, the author of the text must see to it that the elements of the pentad, or the ingredients in the garbage can, are consistent with one another according to the prevailing rules of consistency, in variation of the prevailing rules of consis-tency, or in a meaningful discord with such rules. Thus the emplotment of organization theory may proceed.

A helpful move in this direction might include learning from the detective stories, where the art of plot reached, if not its heights, then at least a level of conscious reflection.

6

Management She Wrote: Organization Studies and Detective Stories

One of the obvious ways to perform a genre analysis is by contrasting an analyzed genre with other genres. I have suggested earlier that novels can become models for organization theory—not for imitation, but for inspiration. They are versions of the world, and, in so far as these are relevant and valid, it is not by virtue of correspondence with 'the world', but by virtue of containing right ('entrenched') categories and of being acceptable (Goodman 1984). Such versions of worlds gain acceptability, not in spite of, but because of, their aesthetic features. It is the power of creative insight and not documentary precision that makes novels both a potential competitor of and a dialogue partner for organization theory.

But the analogy between the novel and organization theory is not well balanced: the novel is a very wide genre, best compared to all social sciences. Organization theory is at best a subgenre in social sciences, and therefore could be fruitfully compared to a subgenre of the novel. Many such comparisons are possible. I have chosen one to concentrate on: the subgenre of the detective story.

WAYS OF WRITING MURDER—AND MANAGEMENT

One striking and specific analogy between detective stories and organization studies is a preference for realist style dictated by an interest in social life. They are both built around problem-solving in a social context. The narratives are constructed in a similar way: there is something amiss, it is neither clear nor obvious what it is (there are many false clues), this 'something' must be explained (the problem must be diagnosed) and—although this is optional in both detective story and organization studies—the way of solving the problem ought to be prescribed. When this last condition is upheld, there is often another striking similarity between the main characters—the detective and the consultant. In case the authorship is hidden, the invisible character of the researcher tells the story, including the solution, without being part of it.

Another analogy concerns the narrative structure, shared by classical detective novels and organization studies. The plot of a detective novel consists of two stories: one is the story of criminal action, which is hidden, and which is revealed through the second story, that of investigation, or acquiring knowledge, which is mystifying to the reader, who does not understand the actions of the detective until the first story is uncovered, and sometimes not even afterwards (Hühn 1987). The story of investigation seems, in a study of an organization, open to the inspection of the reader, as it is clearly demarcated in a chapter or a section entitled 'Method'; however, its highly ritualistic structure is only a different mystifying procedure. Instead of running to and fro with a magnifying glass, the researcher 'applies a technique', and in both cases the reader is left to believe that 'there is a method in this madness'. In the case of the detective story, the actual action is revealed and its underlying pattern is hidden; in the case of an organization study, the pattern is presented as such, but the reader never knows how it was actually applied *in situ*. Both genres often use a variation, including a third story to explicate the second: a naïve observer, like Dr Watson in Sherlock Holmes, who can indulge in stating the obvious, since he has a professional status to save him from a suspicion of lack of intelligence, or a researcher who tells the story of investigation made by a true hero—usually a Leader. The researcher becomes thus a Dr Watson who is protected by the scientific method, and who can safely be in awe of Sherlock Holmes—the practitioner.[1]

Even the readers who became convinced of the correctness of the above analogy, might be put off by the thought of making it. The detective novel is not precisely on the Pantheon of fiction writing. Why compare organization studies to a genre which is by many considered trash, not worthy of a serious reader, on a par with science fiction and only just keeping ahead of cheap romance? There are two famous arguments in defence of the detective story, one formulated by Raymond Chandler from the point of view of the writer, and another formulated by Umberto Eco from the point of view of the reader.

Chandler begins with the somewhat unfortunate statement by Dorothy Sayers (unfortunate for her, as all of Chandler's argument is built up at her expense), according to which the detective story 'does not, and by hypothesis never can, attain the loftiest level of literary achievement' (after Chandler 1950: 191). According to Chandler, there are no criteria of absolute loftiness: 'It is always a matter of who writes the stuff, and what he has in him [this apparently includes Ms Sayers] to write it with. . . . there are no dull subjects, only dull minds' (ibid.). In Chandler's opinion, the greatness of literature is decided by

---

[1]   Keith Hoskins (1996) has another interesting conjecture on this matter. He claims that the prototype of the detective is an academic teacher, with the ultimate right to 'examine'. This model had originated in Edgar Allan Poe's repeated failure in academic examinations, which he revenged inventing a new character—and a new genre.

its realism, in the sense of sociological portrayals of the everyday life of every-day man (yes) in the everyday world. And this is where I see the additional point of convergence between the detective story and organization studies: in both, an exceptional event (murder, loss of profits, decline, fraud) is an inter-ruption that—for a short moment—reveals the well-ingrained structure of the everyday world, which is forgotten and institutionally sealed from inspection in everyday proceedings.

Eco's (1979/1983) argument is somewhat more ambiguous. He claims that most popular fiction earns its appeal thanks to its iterative scheme, thanks to the relaxing redundancy that it provides to cultivated readers, who find in it the well-earned repose from the inquisitive search to which their life is dedicated. Thus even detective stories, which are read supposedly to satisfy the need for surprise and the unexpected, are actually valued for their comforting repeti-tiveness.

Eco's reasoning can be easily paraphrased for the present purpose. Like popular fiction, social-science studies are recognizable—more, defined by—their repetitive structure. Indeed, there is more structural deviance in detective stories than in doctoral dissertations. Whether this iteration offers comfort and relaxation is another matter (although I would claim that it does). But, just as with detective stories, the redundancy can be all that there is, or else the itera-tive scheme and the familiar characters can serve as a stabilizing frame through which to reach novel insights into the complexity of social life, because of the lack of distraction usually produced by structural innovations. In what follows I wish to speak of just such examples of work.

In principle, both detective stories and social-science studies are supposed to build on analytical logic and employ deduction or induction. In practice, formal logic is a rare guest in both. Although Hercules Poirot is supposedly a master of deduction in contrast with Jane Marple's genius of induction, only a very indul-gent reader could actually support this claim. Similarly, Glaser and Strauss (1967), following many other critics of the received theory of knowledge, such as Feyerabend (1956/1988) and Winch (1958), showed convincingly that, although social scientists attempt to use deduction and induction in their approaches, they owe their insights mostly to abduction. It is thus easier to find writings that prescribe the way to proceed deductively or inductively than actual studies that apply analytical logic, especially among those that use field material.

It is abduction, also called the 'logic of discovery', that dominates both genres. The notion of abduction originates in the works of Peirce, his pragma-tism, and his semiotic analysis.

ABDUCTION IN FICTION . . .

Abduction in a detective story is attributed above all to Sherlock Holmes, who collects observations with which he produces a conjecture, a hypothesis, and then experiments, which sometimes leads to refutation of certain elements or the whole hypothesis. Finally he presents the solution to the equally stupefied criminal, Dr Watson, and, sometimes, a police inspector or other witnesses.

It has been suggested that Holmes in fact never verifies his hypotheses, thus failing to follow strict logic and opening himself to a number of parodies that emphasize just this defect (Truzzi 1983). It is an interesting suggestion, which can be seen as correct or incorrect depending on what is assumed to be Holmes's 'method'. If, as suggested by most, it is abduction, there is no need for Holmes to verify his hypotheses—at the point when no refutations occur (and they usually do in the course of detecting), the conclusion can be presented. Besides, as pointed out by Bonfantini and Proni (1983), Holmes uses abduction not to revolutionize general laws, as Peirce suggested, but to arrive at narrow-range theories, theories of a particular case, fitting in well with the received view of the universe. Holmes does 'normal science'.

It is pertinent to notice that, like any researcher, Holmes himself claims he uses strict deduction: 'when this original intellectual deduction is confirmed point by point by quite a number of independent incidents, then the subjective becomes objective and we can say confidently that we have reached our goal'.[2] As in most studies, the talk of 'method' is usually loosely coupled to an actual reporting on the procedure, step by step. When Holmes pontificates about his 'method', Watson is invariably impressed and inscribes it word for word. When Holmes describes what he did, the effect is invariably disillusionment on the part of his public, creating situations like the one in 'The Red-Headed League':

Mr. Jabez Wilson laughed heavily. 'Well, I never!'

'I begin to think, Watson,' said Holmes, 'that I made a mistake in explaining. "*Omne ignotum pro magnifico*", you know, and my poor little reputation, such as it is, will suffer shipwreck if I am so candid.'[3]

Sebeok and Umiker-Sebeok (1983) registered the many ways in which Holmes intentionally mystifies Watson, and made a useful analogy with the medical profession, usually taken as the source of inspiration for the character of Holmes, where a touch of magic in diagnosing supposedly helps recovery. The alleged 'elementary, my dear Watson', albeit non-existent in Doyle's texts, summarizes the usual techniques utilized by experts to put down lay-people. Holmes also shares with the modern scientist the habit of admitting that, although strict deduction is his model, frequent deviations occur: 'One forms provisional theories and waits for time or fuller knowledge to explode them. A bad habit, Mr. Ferguson, but human nature is weak. I fear that your old friend here has given an exaggerated view of my scientific methods.'[4] In other words, a classic case of an aspiring positivist who dabbles in deductive reasoning but depends on abduction for the main result. Where he deviates from the

---

[2]   Arthur Conan Doyle, 'The Adventure of the Sussex Vampire', *The Penguin Complete Sherlock Holmes* (London: Penguin, 1981, 1042).   [3]   Ibid. 177.
[4]   'The Adventure of the Sussex Vampire', ibid. 1038–9.

research model is, as I said before, in actual step-by-step reporting of his deeds and thoughts.

One could make a conjecture that the reason why Holmes now and then reveals his procedure, although it is invariably ridiculed by his public and requires an intensification of mystification attempts, is that Doyle needs to show it to the reader. There is no such need when presenting a doctoral dissertation, although such stories often give color to informal seminars and talks with friends. Attempts to legitimize them by introducing them into the main discourse of the dissertation, although recently more frequent, bristle with difficulties (see Ashmore 1989).

The procedure and the method reflect not only the habits of the scientific community then and now, but also a certain way of seeing the world, a certain cosmology, which Holmes and social scientists share, to a degree. In many analyses of Holmesian detection a parallel is made between the detective and the physician, and through it a generalization is reached concerning the 'useful sciences' (such as law and medicine, although management sciences can easily be included in this group). This is what Ginzburg calls 'an attitude oriented towards an analysis of individual cases, reconstruable only through traces, symptoms, indices' (1983: 109, trans. BC). Sherlock Holmes is interested in society, but society is accessible to him through the minute and multiple inscriptions it makes on individuals, together with biology. The dedication in reading those signs makes him, in the eyes of the critic, an admirable semiotician. As far as organization studies are concerned, here is where the qualifier I used before—'to a degree'—most strongly applies. Many organization studies share with the Holmesian approach the belief that individuals are the only accessible study object, but not necessarily the understanding and the devotion of a semiotician. The obvious is a red rag to Holmes's eyes, but it is—more often than not—taken as obvious in organization studies.

. . . AND IN ORGANIZATION STUDIES

Alvin Gouldner's *Patterns of Industrial Bureaucracy* (1954) begins, as it should, with a description of a disturbance in the existing social order by a demise: premodern, 'organic solidarity', which previously ruled Gypsum Plant, is killed. Modern, industrial bureaucracy is introduced in its place. The issues to detect are several: is this a crime, a demeanor, or just a death from old age? And who, among the suspects, is the real perpetrator: the new plant manager, the new social order, or the Zeitgeist? The detective, called in by the head office, as it seems, is a team of undergraduate students and their tutor, most of them ex-GIs (just as in Holmes's stories, where most of Watson's chums are ex-military).[5] The

---

[5]   For the record, although one woman joined the team at a later stage, it was an all-male operation, including the bonding between the miners and the researchers. And so are Sherlock Holmes stories: women have quite a defined role there, and never that of a detective or his assistant.

reader is informed that the study has been guided by a deductively derived (from Weber's theory of bureaucracy) hypothesis, but the detectives emphasize the openness of their methods, so that no relevant information could escape them (which, as in Holmes's case, will cost them many an apology . . .).

In the process of detection, many interesting details of local and universal folklore are detected—and created: the miners' tales, familiarizing the danger in their jobs, but also 'a Rebecca myth', a Daphne du Maurier metaphor that the researchers pick up to throw light on their findings.

From many tales, observations, and reflections, emerges a picture of two distinct groups: 'the miners', representing and maintaining the old, organic solidarity, and 'the surface', which is already much more bureaucratic when the central events begin. The informal solidarity of the miners is produced both by the spatial arrangement of their jobs, and the constant threat they experience. This, in a sense, justifies their resistance to bureaucracy. On the other hand, they are perceived by the management as unreliable (high levels of absenteeism, due partly to their drinking and gambling habits), and thus in need of bureaucracy. Here, the readers have an opportunity to see how abduction works in practice:

Did this perception of undependability of the miners' work *attendance* arouse bureaucratic efforts, which our hypothesis as presently formulated would imply, and if not, why not? An illuminating example was the case of the 'no-absenteeism' rule. Supervisors in the mine did, at first, attempt to enforce this rule. Very shortly thereafter, however, they bowed to strong informal opposition and declared that this rule just could not be enforced in the mine. . . . This suggests the following modification in our original hypothesis: Even if supervisors see subordinates as failing in the performance of their role, obligations, the adoption of bureaucratic solutions will depend, in part, upon an estimate of whether they will *work*. The mine supervisors had to ask themselves, would the introduction of bureaucratic discipline into the mines, and an emphasis on strict conformity to work regulations, *succeed here*?

There were important features of the mining situation which made supervisors decide that question in the negative. . . . Management's conception of the miners encouraged them to accept the *status quo* in the mine, *forestalling* efforts at bureaucratization, however desirable these might seem.   (Gouldner 1954: 142–3)

Lest it be thought that I am forcing the analogy of the detective pursuit on an unwilling author, here is Gouldner's introduction to the last part of the book:

In seeking to account for the development of bureaucracy we have, so far, conformed to the time-honored canons of the working detective; that is, we sought to demonstrate first, the 'motives', and then the 'opportunity'. In considering the first, it has been suggested that the 'motives' comprise an effort to solve the problem of worker 'apathy'; in examining the 'opportunity', attention has been given to the recalcitrance of the human material, and to the question of whether the 'victim' is cussedly resistant or quietly acquiescent.

By analogy, we are not so much interested in the 'crime' as in the career of the criminal, and this, of course, is shaped by more than his motives or opportunities. It depends also on what happens in the course of such a career. Whether the criminal escapes or is caught is no petty detail; whether he satisfies his motives or frustrates them influences the development of his career.   (Gouldner 1954: 157–8)

'The criminal' is bureaucratic patterns, of course. And now to another piece of analogy, the chapter on method. True to form, the 'Appendix' mixes the description of the actual procedure with apologies for its constant deviation from the 'scientific method':

The purpose of this appendix is not to show how our procedures conformed to the canons of scientific method, but to describe in some detail what we actually did and how we did it. This does not mean that we were insensitive to methodological requirements. As the contrast between mine and surface may indicate, we tried to orient ourselves to the *logic* of controlled experiment—at least as much as our recalcitrant research predicament would permit. Our case study, however, is obviously not a venture in validation. Instead, it is primarily exploratory and comprises an effort to develop new concepts and hypotheses which will lend themselves to validation by experimental methods.   (Gouldner 1954: 247)

One wonders whether they really believed that a 'validation by experimental methods' was possible. At any rate, the conclusions, as usual in detective stories, involve a redefinition of the problem and, as usual, the research team knew that from the very beginning (see Gouldner 1954: 145 n.). With deference to tradition, I will abstain from revealing the conclusions in detail: suffice it to say that they had considerable influence on the ways of seeing bureaucracy in the years to come. Not so the study pattern, though: Gouldner's efforts, like Melville Dalton's later, were much lauded and little imitated. But my choice of this study had little to do with its being typical. It is not that most or even many organization studies resemble Sherlock Holmes stories. The point is that an organization study *might* resemble the Sherlock Holmes story. The final reason why my choice fell on Gouldner is namely that it *reads* like a detective story, it engages and fascinates the reader. The appropriate language games are in place, ensuring the pleasure of an iterative scheme, but there is also mystery.

Old-fashioned mystery, I admit. Nowadays there are other ways of writing detective stories, and doing organization studies.

POSTMODERN(IST) OPTIONS IN DETECTIVE FICTION . . .

The genre of the detective stories seemed to become stale and rigid in the 1920s and the 1930s, when the attempts of genre analysis led to establishing canonical rules, used to discipline the new adepts by the established figures such as S. S. Van Dine or Ronald Knox (Hühn 1987). Chandler spoke with spite of 'a few badly scared champions of the formal or the classic mystery who think no story is a detective story which does not pose a formal and exact problem and arrange the clues around it with neat labels on them' (1950: 197). But, as it can be said that impressionism was produced by the French Academy (which by consistent rejection of paintings not conforming to the rules provoked the opening of the Independent Salon), so one can claim that the rigidification of the rules of the genre made the transgressions easier. Thus the emergence of the 'hard-boiled' novel, whose foremost representative, Dashiell Hammett, is now celebrated as one of the first postmodern writers. Before engaging in unpacking this claim, a brief look at the meaning of this ambiguous adjective might be useful.

The adjectives 'postmodern' and 'postmodernist' have been among the most used in social-science and humanities writing in the 1990s. Sometimes they stand contrasted to 'modern' and 'modernist', sometimes not; sometimes they are used synonymously, sometimes not. I have no ambition to sort out the semantic confusion once and for all, but I wish to propose a temporary order for the purposes of this text. I shall use the word 'postmodern' to denote a special kind of attitude, a sensibility that has its roots in one or another kind of disenchantment with what Lyotard (1979/1987) calls 'The Modern Project'. It comes in two versions: a despairing and a celebratory one. The former concentrates on a feeling of disorientation, meaninglessness, and fragmentation (Wilson 1991). The latter is an attitude of skepticism towards the solutions of modernism ('more control, better control') combined with the realization that actions aimed at wringing order out of disorder seem to be necessary, albeit they are at best only temporarily successful. In other words, it is an attitude of an observer who sees the paradoxicality of life and yet, as an actor, bravely engages in daily efforts to deparadoxify (Luhmann 1991) with not too many expectations of predictable results and lasting effects, and the acceptance of the inevitability of unexpected consequences.

The term 'postmodernist' will be used below in the narrow meaning of a literary form of aesthetic sensibility, developed as a follow-up and on the basis of, modernism as a trend (Fokkema 1984).

There are many points of connection between the two. To begin with, one can claim that postmodern sensibility produced postmodernism. But the two do not coincide completely: postmodern sensibility can find expression in surrealism, magic realism, modernism (see, for example, a plea for 'modernist anthropology' (George E. Marcus 1992)), and, in its celebrating version, in many such forms at once (of which the best example is provided by the works of Paul Auster).

There exists an interesting attempt to read the detective novel as a quasi-postmodernist genre—namely, as an exercise in deconstruction (Hühn 1987). As mentioned before, classical detective fiction contains at least two stories: that of a crime and that of an investigation. If one takes a detective as reader, as Hühn does, the criminal is an author who then tries to write another story—composed of false clues—to cover up the original one, which is inscribed in various material traces of the crime. The detective has to deconstruct the false story—being especially aware of all kind of institutionalized reasoning. The criminal is usually a master of *enthymeme*: leaving cues that should be completed in a certain—misleading—whole while hiding the premises.

The process of deconstruction is hampered on at least two sides. There are, on the one side, other authors, guilty not of a crime in question, but of something else which they wish to conceal, and they either corroborate the criminal's story or write other false stories that must be deconstructed as well. On the other side, there is a competitive reader—the police—who is inept in deconstruction and attempts to close the text before its possibilities have been explored.

The detective differs from a deconstructivist mostly in one respect: refusing to admit the infinity of possible deconstruction and insisting on reconstruction of the 'only true story', thus heeding the demands of a conventional analysis. Even at that point, notes Hühn, the realist stance is somewhat weak: rather than presenting 'the evidence', the detective presents yet another narrative, revealing the ultimate faith in the constituting power of the narrative.

There was, however, one author of detective stories whose anti-classic attitude became in time read as a forerunner of a postmodern attitude and a postmodernist kind of writing: Dashiell Hammett. The postmodern attitude is the way in which his characters conceive of the social life in which they participate. The most cited example (Steven Marcus 1974; Parker 1988) is the case of Flitcraft, a tale that Spade tells Birgit O'Shaughnessy in 'The Maltese Falcon' in order to explain his way of seeing the world.

The tale could have been used by Zygmunt Bauman (1992) to illustrate his concept of a postmodern identity: it is the story of a man who, prompted by a chance event, understood that the way he lived—ordered, rational, and moral—did not correspond with the nature of existence that is 'opaque, irresponsible, and arbitrary' (Steven Marcus 1974: p. xvii). Flitcraft abandoned his previous existence, wandered aimlessly around the world, and then established a new life, taking on the name of Charles Pierce (which, says Marcus, can hardly be a randomly chosen name), then re-created his life as it was before. Here, says Marcus,

we come upon the unfathomable and most mysteriously irrational part of it all—how despite everything we have learned and everything we know, men will persist in behaving and trying to behave sanely, rationally, sensibly and responsibly. And we will continue to persist even when we know that there is no logical or metaphysical, no discoverable or demonstrable reason for doing so.   (Steven Marcus 1974: xviii)

Whereas at this point Marcus himself seems to be on the verge of a metaphysical insight about the 'irreversible and inscrutable human nature', one can point out, in accordance with the argument in this book, that what Flitcraft/Pierce discovers is the futility of the correspondence theory of truth, and the convenience of living according to a story that has an institutional legitimacy in a given time and place. A person living randomly in a world constructed by people who value rationalism may find it rewarding—if, like Hammett (according to Marcus), he or she finds complexity, ambiguity, and paradoxicality pleasurable. Otherwise such a person might find it more practical to adjust to the dominant story of the time, as Flitcraft did. The insight may, after all, not concern the nature of anything—world or people—but the status of knowledge and its uses. And from this perspective, although the main structure of Hammett's stories runs along the genre lines as sketched above, his detectives are consistent deconstructionists, to the bitter end.

Hammett's detective encounters at the outset a 'reality' as accounted for by the others, which, however, soon shows the traces of the fabrication process that went into its production: inconsistencies, lack of coherence, multiple voices selling different versions and adjusting them all the time. The detective sets out to deconstruct those fictions and arrive, true to the ethos of the genre, at the 'true' story. But this final story happens to be just the last story of the text, no more true or plausible than the multitude of versions spun all through the text. This final version seems to fit the detective and his present conditions best, is most feasible, or simply is good enough: the pragmatic attitude is clear. A postmodern anti-hero applies postmodernist skills in his reading/writing activity of the detective. Behind a fiction there is always another fiction—it is the turtles all the way down.

Postmodernist before his time, Hammett presented a problem to his readers, and even to his pupils. His most ardent follower, Raymond Chandler, could not accept the final ambiguity of Hammett's texts and the denial of the role of the 'harbinger of Truth':

> But all this (and Hammett too) is for me not quite enough. . . . In everything that can be called art there is a quality of redemption. It may be pure tragedy, if it is high tragedy, and it may be pity and irony, and it may be the raucous laughter of the strong man. But down these mean streets a man must go who is not himself mean, who is neither tarnished nor afraid. The detective in this kind of story must be such a man. He is the hero, he is everything. . . . The story is this man's adventure in search of a hidden truth and it would be no adventure if it did not happen to a man fit for adventure. . . . If there were enough like him, I think the world would be a very safe place to live in, and yet not too dull to be worth living in.   (Chandler 1950: 197–9)

This is a cry of a romantic against the seeming acceptance of the wrongs of the world by a postmodern hero, a nostalgia for a Superman. Chandler himself did not create such a hero, because his penchant for parody prevented him from this: even in *The Big Sleep* his hero is somewhat like Rex Stout's Archie Goodwin. But recently another pupil of Hammett's created such a person, although she happens to be a woman: this is V. I. Warshawski, Sara Paretsky's creation.

Warshawski defies easy classification: an ardent deconstructivist, a skillful saboteur of the chauvinist language, she nevertheless presents a basically modern attitude: the world is run and distorted by the rich, and the truth lives on the side of the underdogs. But she does not restore order in the world by finding 'the truth' of a case; the world remains as is, which puts V. I. into a bad mood then directed at her friends and people dear to her.

V. I.'s stories make explicit and premeditated the variation of the genre initiated by Hammett's stories in a way unparalleled in all Hammett's other followers. The detective's reading of the crime story changes the story, and changes the detective herself (Hühn 1987). Being on the side of the underdogs and therefore morally right, she nevertheless implicates herself in the story, becoming at least implicitly guilty and sometimes explicitly criminal in her own actions. As Hühn put it, speaking of Hammett's heroes, 'the influence this has on his self-image together with the insight into the inextricably complex ramifications of the crimes tends to produce frustration and disillusionment in him, which finally leave him in a paralyzed state of profound weariness and melancholy' (1987: 461). V. I., however, having invested in a postmodern capacity for self-reflection, knows very well what is ailing her, and therefore takes a bath, a whisky, soaks her battered body and conscience, and starts anew.

Melancholy and disillusionment are, as we said at the outset, only some of the possible consequences of a postmodern attitude. Carl Hiaasen is as much socially sensitive as Sara Paretsky, and each of his books is a small sociological treatise on some kind of societal wrong. His characters, men and women alike, do not bother to fret about the hopelessness of society and its disorders—they take them for a fact. Keen not so much on restoring justice, which they do not see as an original state of affairs in any case, they do not differentiate between crime and non-crime, between what is legitimate or illegitimate, but employ any means, the more outrageous the better, in order to fight against what they consider an ultimate outrage. Nor are they lonely heroes—there is always a small 'interpretive community' who reads the wrongs of the world in the same way and who is equally disenchanted with the legitimate means of protest. The best example is a character who is present in many stories, the ex-governor of Florida who was completely powerless in his post, but as Skink, living on the edge of society, he is able, with the help of other people who think alike, to prevent much crime and injustice—by perpetuating more crime. The reader is forever on a roller coaster—first laughs, then glimpses the massacre caused by these peculiar do-gooders, but then continues to laugh again.

Hiaasen's textual strategies may prove too advanced for organization studies, although the use of irony and absurdity could be much increased. But it is still V. I. Warshawski who may serve as a realistic model for an organization researcher, who, after all, would usually like to see the world somewhat better, but cannot avoid noticing that all the changes for the better are at best limited. When siding with the rulers, the diligent student of organizations cannot but notice that there are victims on the opposite side; while siding with the underdogs, such a student notices, like Burawoy (1979) and Kunda (1992) did, that power also has its complications. They all share a general solicitude for the Other, an understanding of entrapment *and* liberation possibilities provided by the language, and a skepticism towards the Modern Project that would fix all the wrongs of the world once and for all in the march of Progress.

. . . AND IN TEXTS ON ORGANIZATIONS

The two examples I have chosen, Richard Pascale's 'Perspectives on Strategy: The Real Story Behind Honda's Success' (1984) and Marta Calás and Linda Smircich's 'Voicing Seduction to Silence Leadership' (1991), share quite a few similarities but also reveal instructive differences, partly because of the time lag (many mores changed during the seven intervening years).

Pascale begins with Webster's definition of 'strategy', only to move from it to a more pragmatic view that emphasizes varying uses of the word relative to the cultural context. While the concept acquired quite a special meaning in the Anglo-Saxon world of management, this use, and the notion as such, is alien in the Japanese context. Consequently, the application of the notion on events and developments taking place in a non-Anglo-Saxon world becomes a peculiar operation, which is the focus of Pascale's article.

In the Boston Consulting Group's rendition of Honda's entry into the US market, the company's success is explainable in terms of their strategy. 'Honda is portrayed as a firm dedicated to being the low price producer, utilizing its dominant market position in Japan to force entry into the U.S. market, expanding that market by redefining a leisure class . . . segment, and exploiting its comparative advantage via aggressive pricing and advertising' (Pascale 1984: 51).

Pascale confronts this story with one produced by himself in a group interview with the six Japanese executives responsible for the events that took place in 1959. 'The story that unfolded . . . highlights miscalculation, serendipity, and organizational learning—counterpoints to the streamlined "strategy" version related earlier' (p. 51).

It does indeed: here follows a funny story of blunders, chance happenings and sheer persistence. Enough to say that, while the (then) young executives were trying to sell larger bikes, their future hit—the 50cc—became known to the public only because they used them as a cheap means of transportation when destitute in Los Angeles.

The use to which Pascale put the two contrasting stories oscillates between 'the old' and 'the new' style of organization studies. On the one hand, he says that both stories are valuable; on the other, he proceeds to choose the second as 'most appropriate in the environmental context of the eighties' (p. 57) on the basis of another streamlined story, this time produced by himself. On the one hand, he criticizes the traditional theory for its simplifications and reductionism, for its ignorance of 'the givens of organizations' that are 'ambiguity, uncertainty, imperfection, and paradox' (p. 65). On the other, he mainly proposes to extend the list of the determining factors from one item (strategy) to six (the 'excellence' list of 6 Ss), which should take care of everything, ambiguity and paradox included. Finally, the sub-title itself—the 'real' story—suggests a powerful commitment to the idea that there is one story that is 'truer' than all the others—or, perhaps, that six stories are truer than one.

These oscillations are absent from Calás and Smircich's work. Here, the 'text detectives' make perhaps their first appearance in organization studies. 'Reality' is a moot point in this exercise: interesting readings of well-known texts are the point. Unlike Pascale, who represented 'the truth', the two authors have a 'standpoint', which is a feminist one.

As in Pascale's text, a dictionary makes an appearance early in the text, but in a role that has become paradigmatic since. The lexical quotes attempt neither to establish 'the accurate meaning of the word' nor, as in Pascale's text, to contrast the dry simplification of a dictionary with living usage (which builds a parallel to the contrast between the 'Honda strategy' and 'Honda real' stories). They serve as a brief review of the history of uses ('genealogy'), sedimented in etymology, 'witnesses', as it were. Calás and Smircich then reread four classical texts on leadership in terms of . . . seduction.

Is their 'seduction' reading of the texts 'truer' than the 'leadership' one? Certainly not, especially as this criterion does not carry much relevance in the present context. 'Truer' to what? Authors' intentions? Yes and no, as Mintzberg's (1991: 602) agitated answer indicated: he refused 'leadership as seduction', but admitted 'writing as seduction', making the detectives into perpetrators, another typical turn of fate for a postmodern detective. As literary theory taught us a while ago, however, if readers were constrained by authors' intentions, the whole civilization would not get very far. Luckily for both the authors and the readers, the writers write more than they know.

Is, then, 'seduction' a complementary perspective that, together with 'leadership', will tell us all about organizations? Again, although Pascale and Calás and Smircich make a seemingly identical point about the value of multiplicity of perspectives/meanings, the consequences are not the same. For Pascale, six is better than one, but six happen to exhaust the interpretive possibilities (a lucky number?). For Calás and Smircich, the readings are endless; in fact, they continue with three 'utopias' that are in a sense 'further' readings, beyond the edge of what is (organization literature). There is an interesting spatial parallel in Pascale's and Calás and Smircich's percourses. He stops at Peters and Waterman, who provide the answer to all his troubles. They put Peters and Waterman just before the edge (sitting safely on the mainland, as it were), and then cross the edge, leaving Peters and Waterman behind.

The readings are endless only in principle; in practice, as pointed out many a time, and most convincingly as regards the social sciences by Ashmore (1989), the fear of 'endless semiosis' or 'aporia' is greatly exaggerated. The institutional frame of time and space limits the repertoire pretty much, and such social mechanisms as fashion and imitation introduce further limitations (for example, they seem to have chosen the 'untrue' Honda's story instead of Pascale's). The organization-theory detectives do not claim that two stories are twice as good as one; it is just that they cannot help noticing many stories always floating around, which makes suspense greater rather than less. Too great, as some readers claim.

How do these two organizational texts compare with the detective stories mentioned above? Hiaasen's heroes and heroines, upon discovering a version of a story that contradicts the official one, commit outrages; Pascale runs for help to 'normal science' (the police?), choosing to fit his discovery to the legitimate frame, rather than trying to break the frame. Calás and Smircich commit an outrage, just as V. I. Warshawski would do. Like her, they are engaged in a relentless battle against gender-discrimination crimes committed in language. The difference between Warshawski and Calás and Smircich is that she is also an ethnographer, documenting a new angle of contemporary life in all her adventures. In this sense, she is closer to such organizational detectives as Gideon Kunda (1992) and Robin Leidner (1993). After all, a genre is a space, not a point. How does it look, however, when the time dimension is added? A large shift occurred between the Pascale and Calás and Smircich articles. What can we expect of the future? After all, genre analysis is dynamic: it registers the emergence of genres, their transformations, and possible deaths.

WHO, IF NOT THE BUTLER?

It has been claimed, in fact, that the postmodern detective story is a harbinger of its own demise. Although the detective

is frequently still able to read the truth in the text, he can no longer extract it, as it were, and employ it to remedy injustice and disorder in society. In short, he cannot publish the story anymore . . . the truth is useless and ineffectual, because society is not interested in finding the hidden meaning, nor is there a general consensus about the necessity of detection at all. . . . The detective reading venture is thus no longer supported or even legitimized by an interpretive community. The story has lost its social function and potential power.   (Hühn 1987: 461–2)

Hühn's reading, so close to Chandler's lament above, collapses the fate of the detective into the fate of the detective story. Is this justified? It is certainly correct, as Jon Thompson (1993) pointed out, that, while the modern detective traded knowledge for power, the postmodern detective earns only confusion in this transaction. But why should the powerlessness of the detective equal the powerlessness of the genre? The market success of Paretsky and Hiaasen, to name only two, tells quite a different story. In fact, Hiaasen's heroes and heroines do remedy justice and disorder in society in their peculiar, hard-boiled way. One could rather speak of a revival and a renewal within the genre: Hammett, a marginal phenomenon in the times of Doyle and Christie, is situated by his followers in the mainstream, in the center. What is more, the 'high-culture' fiction seems to be approaching this popular genre rather than distancing itself from it.

With its origins attributed to Borges, a subgenre of 'metaphysical detective story' is emerging (Rowen 1991). Contemporary works such as Paul Auster's *City of Glass*, Patrick Süskind's *Perfume*, Haruki Murakami's *Hard-Boiled World*, and Jeannette Winterson's *Passion* are all detective stories—in a fashion. They all retain the iterative scheme as a reflexive allusion or a pastiche, and remake the simple mystery, to be straightened out by a clever detective, into the mystery of individual life and social order. At the end, the mystery deepens, if anything, and yet the readers feel richer and wiser, or perhaps just comforted by company.

Rowen, who analyzed Auster's *City of Glass*, points out that Auster's character, Quinn, seeks in the detective story 'a refuge from the metaphysical chaos that he finds around him' (Rowen 1991: 226).[6] What he finds are other people engaged in a similar quest, to the point of self-annihilation. The paradoxical lesson is that looking for final order is nothing but the final madness.

It is not a lesson that is easily transferred to the world of organizations, where the quest for control is still uncurbed. And yet at least some organization theorists point out that such a quest threatens annihilation not only of those who seek it but also of the whole world. One may hope that the two genres will change in the same way, that swift and simple remedies are out of fashion, in detective stories and in organization studies.

Much to my delight, there exist now experiments in 'scientifiction' that are hybrids of two genres, which indicate that this must be the case. Two I wish to mention are Latour's previously discussed *Aramis or the Love of Technology* (1996) and Goodall's *Casing a Promised Land* (1994). In *Aramis*, the Master and his Pupil, modelled, to my eye, most closely on William of Baskerville and Adso in Eco's *In the Name of the Rose*, are given the task of solving the mystery of the death of beautiful Aramis, or the 'Agencement en Rames Automatisées de Modules Indépendants dans les Stations' (the arrangement in automated trains of independent modules in stations). The Master is a sociologist of science and technology, the Pupil is an engineer who takes courses in social sciences at the École des Mines, and Aramis is a piece of transportation machinery, whose cars couple and decouple automatically, following the programming of the passengers. Born in the late 1960s, Aramis promised to be the kind of technology that serves humans and saves environment, and yet in November 1987 it was nothing but a piece of dead machinery in a technology museum.

Who killed Aramis? Engineers? Politicians? Economists? Secret allies? Fate? Hypotheses multiply and the plot thickens.

Goodall's book reminds one more of *The Singing Detective* because of its autobiographical character. Six stories portray six detective adventures of an organizational communication specialist who, by default and by design, enters various organizational settings, looking for clues and reading them. The mystery revealed by degrees is an identity of an organization researcher, spiralling around in the familiar and strange world of US corporations. Is he in or is he out?

---

[6]   It should be pointed out that her reading differs dramatically from that given Auster by the doyen of British crime stories, Julian Symons, who labels *The City of Glass* a 'clever, sterile book' (1992: 267), reading in it a contempt rather than a celebration of the detective-story tradition. In terms of frequency, however, Rowen's reading is more common.

There are many interesting similarities and differences in these two books. They are both placed in technology-intensive settings, and yet, while Latour subject-ivizes things and machines, Goodall does a careful purification work, sifting the human project (symbolization) from the mavericks of objects. Only once does he seem to be on the verge of being seduced by technology: inside the space-shuttle simulator. But then, once again outside, he (and his colleagues, university professors) seem to be ashamed of brushing shoulders with things so closely as to forget what they symbolize.

According to the authors, *Aramis* is a realist work while *Casing a Promised Land* is surrealist. Short of those labels, the reader might easily think that it is the other way around. This teaches a contemporary reader a lesson or two: one is, never believe authors' self-classifications and look for yourself; the other is, that there is a great variety of realisms . . .

A better clue to their differences is to be found in their model detectives. I compared Latour's Master and Pupil to Baskerville and Adso, not only because of the obvious analogy, but also because Baskerville and Adso are themselves repositories of many models of detection. The Master mentions Holmes and Colombo, and incorporates this unlikely mixture of self-assurance and humbleness. Goodall dedicates his work to Raymond Chandler, and indeed there is a similar romanticism and a strong trace of the humanist project in his play with words and events. The Master is truly *past*-modern in his project of embracing the machines with sincere affection, no matter how non-human they are.

What the two works have in common, and what is of utmost relevance for me, is that they are not 'fiction books written by social scientists'. There were many attempts of that kind that ended either with success, thus redefining the scientist as a novelist, or else with failure, which seemed further to prove that the two do not mix. Latour and Goodall do not dabble in fiction: they propose, seriously, and to my mind very successfully, to hybridize the two genres into a new one.

THE FUTURE IS A MYSTERY

The time-honored analogy between the detective and the scientist, pointed out by many authors before me (Nicolson 1946; Porter 1981; Hühn 1987), was supposed to reside in the two characters' common ability to reveal the true meaning, to reaffirm the rule of reason, and to reimpose order on chaos. Hühn suggests that it was actually science that first suffered from the tremors of self-doubt, from the *coup d'état* of relativity, and that the scientists turned to detective stories as the last place where order could be kept in spite of all threats. That might no longer be true, and yet there are still many things to be found in detective stories. After all, as Lyotard pointed out, the demise of meta-narratives—of Progress and Emancipation—makes a lot of room for the little narrative, which 'remains the quintessential form of imaginative invention, most particularly in science' (Lyotard 1979/1987: 61). The postmodern detective story provides an encouraging example showing the variety of experimentation with such 'little narratives' that can be achieved once the rules of the genre are well understood and used—not as a means to control and discipline, but as a springboard for transgression.

Such avant-gardistic ambitions may, however, raise doubts as to whether the management practice, its importance so much emphasized in the beginning of this book, will not fade behind the literary interest of organization studies. In the last chapter I focus, therefore, on issues central to management writing, no matter what plot or style: the issue of representation and the solution of polyphony.

On the Imperative and the Impossibility of Polyphony in Organization Studies

'*La Pologne? La Pologne?* It's very cold over there, isn't it?' the lady asked and sighed with relief. So many new countries have cropped up recently that the weather is the only safe subject for conversation.

'Oh yes, dear,' I wanted to answer her, 'poets have to write in gloves in my country. I won't say they never take them off; they do when the full moon warms them up. They extol the simple life of sealherds in thundering stanzas because nothing less sonorous could overcome the roaring blizzard. Our classics, icicles of frozen ink in hand, carve on snowdrifts stamped smooth. The rest, a bunch of decadents, weep over their bad fortune, their tears little stars of snow. Whoever wants to drown himself, must buy an ax and cut a hole in the ice. That's how it is, dear.'

I wanted to tell her all this. But I forgot the French word for seal. Neither I was sure about icicle and ax.

'*La Pologne? La Pologne?* It's very cold over there, isn't it?'

'*Pas du tout,*' I answered icily. (Szymborska 1978)[1]

Szymborska was, of course, not the only one to suffer from ambiguity created by the existence of many languages. One human dream, especially cherished by science, is that of a state where this uncertainty has been removed. One divine way of achieving such a state is *xenoglossia*, or the possibility of perfect understanding in spite of the multiplicity of languages.[2] The human practice, however, means experiencing constant difficulties of translation. Translation is not something limited to a contact between two languages, but 'is formally and pragmatically explicit in *every* act of communication' (Steiner 1975/1992: p. xii). This means that every organization story, every report on managerial practice, is an act of translation.

An act of translation can be seen as involving *centripetal* (inward) *and centrifugal* (outward) *moves* on the part of the translator, and their consequences can be

An earlier version of this chapter was presented at the EIASM conference 'Organizing in a Multi-Voiced World', Leuven, Belgium, 4–6 June 1997.

¹ This text was translated by Krzysztof Zarzecki as part of the Iowa Creative Writing Program at the University of Iowa (1964).

² This is one way of interpreting the miracle of Pentecost. Another postulates glossolalia—i.e. the gift of tongues, a divinely inspired capacity to talk and understand all languages.

debated not only in literary but in political terms. Translation attempted by an organization researcher acquires the character of a political representation, and this is the second topic I take up. I then turn to the theme of a perfect language, the possibility or impossibility of establishing a frame of reference that would allow evaluation of the faithfulness of translation or the truthfulness of representation. If such a frame is not possible, a Tower of Babel might result; a scenario, I argue, not as undesirable as it may look at first glance. Thus I end by painting a picture of a knowledge bazaar, where all organizational translators might be said to live.

TRANSLATION: HIDING AND REVEALING

While attempting to study power as an experiential concept within the Study of Power and Democracy in Sweden, I collected stories that were supposed to illustrate organizational power from students of management and related disciplines in various countries. I interpreted those texts, written in students' first languages, from various points of view, one of which was the issue, or rather non-issue, of gender. 'Gender is a primary way of signifying relationships of power,' claimed Joan Scott (1986: 1067). Thus, I reasoned, the issue of gender should either appear explicitly in the stories, or else transpire from the events that were reconstructed. I could not locate any such traces in stories coming from German, Swedish, or British students. The Italian and Finnish students, however, mentioned gender as an issue in the context of power, whereas Polish students apparently put some effort into concealing the biological sex of the protagonists in their stories (Czarniawska-Joerges 1994).

I discovered this while trying to handle the (seemingly mundane) task of translating a text written in Polish into English. I realized that, while a stylistic requirement called for the use of a personal pronoun rather than the repetition of a noun, I did not know which pronoun to use. This difficulty occurred rather often: sometimes the gender of the protagonist could be guessed only because the protagonist was identical with the narrator (who indicated her sex in response to a formal request, included in the research format). The gender of the protagonist could be deduced from the gender of verbs and the address used in direct speech (verbs are gendered in Polish). The gender of one of the characters (the Dean's Proxy) became apparent through an address in direct speech, but the gender of the Administrator remained unknown. I will mark these dilemmas in the text by indicating gender in Polish (M, F, or U (unknown)).

Student and the emergency allowance

A student (M) was allocated a flat, but had no money for furniture, additional loans, or other expenses. As he (M) knew about the system of 'emergency allowances', he (M) filled in an application form and went with it to the appropriate office:

STUDENT. **Good morning. This is my application, can I leave it here? (F)**
ADMINISTRATOR. **What application? (U)**

s. For an emergency allowance.

a. And what exactly is the emergency?

s. I've got a flat and . . . (F)

a. That's known as good luck, not an emergency. Emergency means you're a single mother, for example.

s. But . . .

a. There is no but. There is no reason to give you an allowance, so there is no reason to hand in the application.

This conversation took place in the presence of the Dean's Proxy for Student's Affairs.

s. Maybe you (M) could help me? I'm really in a very difficult situation.

p. You've heard what was said, haven't you! There is no justification.

s. But maybe you could at least read my application and give me some advice?

p. There's nothing to advise you about. There are no grounds and that's that.

s. But why?

p. The rules do not allow for it—you can find all the relevant information on the notice board in the corridor.

s. But the rules can't cover all emergency situations!

p. I wouldn't know. The fact is, you have no right to anything.

s. [in desperation]. Can I at least appeal against this decision to the President?

p. You can always appeal. It's your right. But I bet you nothing will happen.

[A. smiles ironically]

My translation bears clear traces of centripetal moves: I have reduced, simpli-fied, and familiarized the text for its intended readers. But it was while I was performing this move that I noticed the incongruency between the Student's gender in the introduction and in direct speech. This in turn made me notice that there was no way to establish the gender of the Administrator. The task of translation opened a necessity of a centrifugal move—I could not make sense of my translation without going outside the text.

These incongruencies concerning gender, I reasoned, may just have been a peculiarity of this story. I reached for other Polish stories and found the same phenomenon. It was most often the person abusing power whose gender was hidden. This observation made me return to the Swedish stories which I had originally judged as not referring to gender, and I concluded that, in fact, gender was carefully hidden in most stories and, because of specifics of the Swedish language, I could not deduce it from any cues. Had it not been for the need of translation, I would never have done such a close reading of these texts.

Whether students hid the gender on purpose or not is not an issue, I decided. They could have done it consciously, thus framing the story, in this case at least, as a serious story of organizational power and not 'a feminist story'. However, it could be that it is the language of organizations (the charac-ters are named by their functions: 'student', 'administrator', 'dean's proxy') that automatically frames the story as gender-less.

I then noticed that the Administrator in the story did exactly the opposite of what the student had done in her account: framed the discourse in terms of gender. The allowance aspect was a pretext for the Administrator to evoke a context that would be humiliating for the student. A single mother in a socialist state had a right to all sorts of allowances, but at the same time it is shameful for a Catholic woman to be a single mother. And, even if the student was not a single mother, she could yet become one by the sheer virtue of her sex.

Why, the reader may well ask, is 'a feminist story' less serious than 'an organizational power story'? To answer this question, I needed to continue my centrifugal move till I found what can be seen as yet another translation problem. Western feminism fell on deaf ears in Central and East European countries because the voice that claimed to be emancipatory sounded the same as the voice of the oppressor. The official propaganda of socialism and the first feminists texts that appeared in Central and Eastern Europe used the same Marxist rhetoric, and, after the first impression had been made, it was too late to point out that this rhetoric was used differently. For those who wanted to turn away from the conservative rhetoric of the Church, there was no alternative rhetoric of solidarity: all loquacious voices belonged to enemies.

The issue is, of course, not limited to Western feminism. Further centrifugal moves are required in order to understand the insistence of such centripetal translations, which are produced by a constant necessity of translating from local to globalized languages and back. Lucy Irigaray asked, for example: 'Is not what we conventionally call our *mother tongue . . .* always indeed paternal?' (1985: 86). Now, who is 'we' and what convention is this? In Polish the expression is precisely 'father's speech'. Irigaray went on saying that, as everything in language must be of feminine or masculine gender, 'our' visions of the world are necessarily geared to this dichotomy. Silvia Gherardi, a native speaker of a non-globalized language, was more perceptive: 'Many languages, Italian, French and Spanish for example, have only two genders, and we Latins live in a world where "things" are either masculine or feminine' (Gherardi 1994: 596). Slavic languages have three genders, and Finnish, I am told, only one. But global languages tend to assume that the reality underpinning their grammar is the expression of universal human nature, of which local variations are just deviations.

There may be traces of even older discourses than that of contemporary feminism and organization theory in the conversation. Maria Janion, in her excellent *Women and the Spirit of Otherness* (1996: 190), pointed out that the women artists and intellectuals at the previous turn of the century painfully realized that their choice is to be 'albo czlowiek, albo kobieta' (either a human being, or a woman (observe that in Polish the noun denoting a man, *mezczyzna*, shares only grammatical gender with the word denoting a human being)). As a part of a programme of 'becoming a human being', they often used depersonalized masculine nouns denoting functions, roles, or professions—Lieutenant, Artist, Scientist, Administrator.

All these glosses explaining the peculiarities of the Polish language and the Polish tradition were centrifugal moves that I was forced to insert to defend the translation against the centripetal force activated by repeated translations from local languages to 'globalized' ones, such as English, but also French or German. Szymborska's drastic and desperate centripetal move in *Words* is by no means a poetic invention. Such translations, MacIntyre (1988) points out, are only possible at all because the local text becomes decontextualized (a historical and local context is often appended as an explanatory gloss). This decontextualization is often plainly clear when a retranslation is done: the local speakers often do not recognize this as an original text. Thus, says MacIntyre (1988: 385):

The task of translation into such a language has been achieved at the cost of producing something which would not be recognized or accepted by speakers and writers for whom the original language-in-use was their first language, but who had learned the particular internationalized language as their second first language.

This distortion by translation out of context from the standpoint of those who inhabit the traditions from which the distorted texts are taken is of course apt to be invisible to those whose first language is one of the internationalized languages of modernity. For them it must appear that there is nothing which is not translatable into their language. Untranslatability—if cautious, they may say untranslatability in principle—will perhaps appear to them as a philosophical fiction.

Those for whom the 'globalized' language has become the second first language are constantly faced with the problem of untranslatability of their own experience. Indeed, it is usual that such translations end with a pathetic coda containing such a statement. What is more, the repeated decontextualization of original texts, which leads to their impoverishment in the 'globalized-language' version, gives rise to a suspicion that one's local culture is indeed less rich than the globalized one, and that, were they on an equal footing, the impoverishment would not occur. Reciprocal translations between two local languages make mutual untranslatability only too obvious; such symmetry does not exist between a local and a globalized language.

When translating from a globalized to a local language, a context is taken together with a text and considered universal. In order to translate Katz and Kahn's *The Social Psychology of Organizations* into Polish, I had to learn a lot about baseball, the then (and now) very exotic game to me, as they chose to use it as a leading metaphor in their book. There is no need to be a translator to know the feeling: while any presentation of a local field study requires thousands of excuses, glosses, and apologies, each of us in organization theory is intimate with details of the most obscure US organizations. A similar phenomenon occurs within national languages, where some group languages are considered universal and others not. The experience with Katz and Kahn helped me to think out a revenge: in my writing, examples are often taken from cooking, sewing, and fashion.

A simple act of translation thus produces a series of contradictory moves and a plethora of consequences. A translation of a local text into a globalized language requires a strong centripetal move, which equals the impoverishment of the text, but at the same time it forces the production of glosses that are clearly centrifugal. Translations from globalized language force an extension of a local language, a centrifugal move, but at the same time produce an impression of the inadequacy of the local language, a centripetal move. This complex process problematizes the role of the translator, whose responsibility is to stand for—that is, to represent—both texts. All these problems, albeit often unacknowledged, are the daily bread of a student of organizations.

TRANSLATION AS REPRESENTATION

Science represents nature—that is, facts and things. Politics and law represent interests—that is, people and culture. This ingenious seventeenth-century distinction, says Latour (1993), who blames it on Boyle and Hobbes, makes us forget that, as the verb these two statements have in common, 'represent', indicates, the same process is in focus: representation. Representing nature or things means that scientists stand in their defence and construct their interests, as is clearly shown by the environmentalist movement. Representing people's interests means that lawyers and politicians reify them for the sake of objectivity and justice. What does organization theory do? Both, although to a great extent inadvertently. When adopting a humanist mantle, it actually reifies people, assuming itself to be a correct reader of what is 'their interest'. When taking on a naturalist stance and presenting organizational life as a series of objective facts, it runs into a problem of 'things talking back'—people under study disagreeing with that 'objective representation'.

On a textual plane, these two moves can be seen again as centripetal and centrifugal. Any attempt to tell a coherent story of organizing can be seen as a centripetal move: away from details, richness, variety to be encountered in the field. Any attempt to embellish the story with details, any 'thick description', ends as a centrifugal move: conclusions belie the quotes they follow, coherence and relevance pale and vanish. 'There is a centrifugal impulse in the language', says George Steiner (1992: 33), but there is a centripetal imperative in science.

Let me illustrate this with an example of a business conversation that I first recorded and then interpreted (that is, translated from a natural language to a scientific one).

A business conversation

The conversation below took place between a representative of a water utility company from Mining Town, a representative of a Foreign Company that cooperates with that utility, and a representative of a Warsaw Waterworks, for whose benefit the presentation was made.

MINING TOWN. *Our enterprise does not yet have a legal form, but we already have the letter of intent and our intention is to create a company within a year. Twenty per cent of the Mining Town Waterworks have been sold and by the end of this month 51 per cent of it will have been bought by its employees or by the people who used to work for the company. We are the first water utility to be privatized directly. The municipality takes care of the sales, whereas we take care of operations and construction. It is the [Foreign Company's hometown] model. There is a kind of hat that is municipal, whereas all that could be privatized has been turned over to companies, which are simply the contractors for the purchaser of the services.*

WARSAW WATERWORKS. And how does it work from the point of view of the users?

MT. The key matter concerns the way in which prices are determined. We do not produce water, we buy it from the Town. Therefore, the first element of cost is the purchase of water, and in this case the rate is determined by the county governor. The second element of cost is the value of our work, that is, the maintenance of the efficiency of the town's water network and sewage. Their inspectors control us. Every single event in the field is evaluated financially.

WW. The control network must be very extensive.

MT. Madam, there are only fifteen people. Only fifteen people control our entire company. It is computers that control us, not people. I also had thought that the control machinery would be huge, but it is not. I have a contract with the Town. The contract defines the rules, so you can calculate and control in many ways, but there is a set of fixed conditions, and the fundamental condition is a constant supply of water . . . In the case of a breakdown, we deliver water in water wagons.

WW. With every breakdown? How uneconomical!

MT. You have to remember that a breakdown in our town can last up to eight hours. In Mining Town it is a different story from Warsaw. Cast iron pipes can break at the stamp of a foot and it is impossible to imagine the town without water for that long. Reality forces this kind of solution on us.

WW. And what about complaints and the division of responsibility between the two companies?

MT. No such problem exists. It is a different organizational model. Every time the so-called primary layer, that is, the surface, gets ripped, for us the end of fixing damage is when this primary layer is reinstated as it was. It means making a road accessible, making a lawn or whatever it might be usable. We use a block method. Block A is my company, and a block B is a subcontractor who removes the effects of the damage.

WW. Has it never happened that this subcontractor did not start on time, forgot some-thing, or did a bad job? [WW lists here the so-called pains of socialism.]

MT. No, it has never happened, at least in the past three years.

WW. But during winter it might happen that you work for a few weeks, then all of the sudden everything freezes and you have to stop. I cannot believe that your subcon-tractor will not sometimes forget that there is an unfinished job.

MT. No way [he quotes examples of spectacular emergencies that were taken care of in an equally spectacular way]. *On average we have fifteen such cases a day, but you have to remember that the mining industry in our area does incredible things. I will show you the report for the last quarter.* [He consults his Time Manager] . . . *Now I found it! Six hundred breakdowns in the first quarter.*

WW. The costs must be enormous.

MT. Oh yes, I know, my colleagues from other towns come and wring their hands in despair, saying that it is impossible to work like this.

FOREIGN COMPANY. Tell the director how much the water and the sewage cost.

MT. Our operational costs are the lowest in the region because of this kind of organiza-tional solution.

WW. How do you know that your costs are the lowest?

MT. Because until 1990 the enterprise in Mining Town had nineteen plants with a central supply system, all of which had had an identical organization and management system. So now, when they have been separated, it is easy to compare. [He tells the story of their transformation.]

    In Katowice there are also three enterprises that have been transformed in much the same way as we were. Is this a good model? Well, we are being evaluated by a French consulting company, in other words, by a third party.

ww. [somewhat defensively]. *The water and sewage problems are different in different regions and it is impossible to deal with them in the same way.*

MT. *I do agree. I am not saying that they should, not really. I am just telling you that we are simply doing our job. We live and we want to survive.*

ww. *Well, with such an energetic and dynamic manager!*

FC. *You can see it right away, can't you?* [Turns to the manager.] *Tell the director also about our forms of financing, what kind of proposals we have when we submit our tenders, and what kind of services we offer.*

MT. *When consumers did not want to pay . . . you must know that there was a philosophy between those state giants that water is not a product but a common good. Thus, they decided that we would give them credit anyhow because they have to live, and everybody knows that without them the region would not survive. So we had to find a solution to this financial jam, and we did it through a special marketing idea. Whenever we have difficulties in collecting payment from a consumer, we propose alternative forms of payment. For example, we take coal, steel, energy, and industrial products. We belong to a network of auction firms.*

ww. [feigning surprise]. *And what firm does all that?*

MT. *Ours. The Water and Sewage Works.*

ww. *You should change the name.* (laughs)

MT. *But why? We do what we are able to do. We sell our services even beyond the city limits, because we have to find resources to do our job.*

. . .

ww. *And how is life in Silesia in general?*

MT. *Really awful. We would not even touch this debt business, because it is so tiresome. We have a production team and a financial and marketing team, just to survive.*

ww. *When the situation improves, you will, of course, fire them.*

FC. *Not at all. We will school them for another job.*

MT. *Right now, we have the opposite problem. Good marketing people are being stolen from us. The Mining Town Municipal Enterprise itself steals them.*

ww. *Well, I also forced my employees to do many things, but I did not get as far as marketing.* [General laughter]

(O64)

And now this is what I have done with it.

Researcher's interpretation

What Mining Town is presenting here, with open pride, is the so-called purchaser–supplier model, in which the purchaser is also a company, but a non-profit one, directly responsible to the Town Council. This kind of solution was popular in Scandinavia during the early 1990s.

This kind of self-presentation, which undoubtedly bears the hallmarks of self-promotion, is something rarely seen in the Polish organizational context. It explains the scepticism of WW and the 'prompting' by FC, who checks whether 'the script' is adhered to.

The echo of traditional animosity toward 'trade' as opposed to 'production' is audible in this conversation. Prus wrote about it in 1864 in The Doll. *It is not an exclusively historical animosity, though, or exclusively Polish for that matter. Financial business—that is, 'earning money from money'—is the target of animosity not only because of historical and cultural considerations, but also because it saps many manufacturing fields and trades of importance and their professional pride.*

There were many threads in this conversation that returned in other contexts. The typical share of problems with debtors had led to a search for a survival strategy or even to an improvement in the financial situation by assuming the debts and the resulting diversification of activities. In such a situation various other problems arose, such as the turn away from a professional tradition ('water people' should work with water), or a breach of society's trust (how can one gain profit from the common good such as the water?). Behind the historical animosity towards transactions of purely financial nature lurks also a modernistic fondness for purity—in terms of specialization, as Latour (1993) would have called it.

The interpretation is a clear example of a centripetal move. The conversation became drastically reduced in space (and therefore in attention). There were many more topics taken up in this conversation than those I took up, and the topics I selected were most likely of minor importance, if of any importance at all, for the participants. After all, this was a business conversation whose main point was, would Waterworks buy Mining Town services or not? This is, however, hardly *my* main point.

Last but not least, my interpretation wiped out all 'dialects' present in the conversation. There was the power dialect: the Waterworks' Director was the most powerful participant in the conversation, and she exploited it, sometimes on the verge of rudeness. This was met by a 'teflon attitude' from the Mining Town manager, who did not react to any bait but continued selling his pitch. What is more, the Director was a woman, while the two other participants were men—a situation that was clearly more uncomfortable to Foreign Company than to Mining Town. Further, Waterworks and Mining Town were Poles, whereas Foreign Company was a foreigner, and his Polish was correct but stilted. Finally, Waterworks and Foreign Company represented the big cities and the big world, while Mining Town was an exotic province ('how is life in Silesia?'). The dynamics caused by these various allegiances and resulting in changing temporary affiliations was left out of my interpretation. Obviously, these were not the topics of my study, but did I represent the voices of the field as is my alleged duty?

I can, however, also show examples of my centrifugal moves. To begin with, the whole conversation was inserted in a text, and contained various hints that allowed the readers to observe this interplay of dialects. Also, my interpretation opened a dialogue with other conversations: for example, the one concerning the usefulness of the purchaser–supplier model in the public sector, or that concerning the supposed modernity of contemporary organizations.

As I see it, the analysis adopted in my study consisted of setting up a conversation between various texts that otherwise might never have been spoken to one another. This happens, of course, in a complete contravention of ideal speech conditions—I forced them to speak to each other on my conditions, with myself drawing the conclusions and having the last word. What, then, about my expected commitment to the voices from the field?[3]

The problem of voices in field studies was perhaps most sharply focused in anthropology.[4] 'The gap between engaging others where they are and representing them where they aren't, always immense but not much noticed, has suddenly become extremely visible' (Geertz 1988: 130). After decades of all-knowing anthropological texts that explained the 'native ways of being' to the 'more developed civilization', a wave of political and ethical doubts pervaded the discipline. One representative of reflective anthropology was Stephen Tyler (1986), who opted for a different, polyphonic ethnography, in which people could speak in their own voices. This led to much discussion about whether it was in fact possible. Another member of the same group, George Marcus, writing in 1992, renamed postmodern ethnography as 'modernist' (in a tribute to the 1920s movement) and claimed that, in spite of many obvious problems, one must try to approach at least a semblance of polyphony.

A French literary theorist, Philippe Lejeune (1989), pointed out that the notion of the 'ethnological gap' arose in the first place in relation to cultures where speech went 'before writing'. This gap seemed enormous, and the optimists looked forward to diminishing it by increasing literacy. This achieved, the gap changed into a gap of 'different languages', aggravated by political and moral animosities towards Western dominance. Lejeune took up yet another case—namely, that of representing those who, for instance, read but do not write—for example, the working class. He showed many interesting examples of workers who became writers, thus ceasing to be workers and keeping the gap intact. Writers belong among the intellectuals, no matter where they come from, who they pose as, or what social group they are writing about.

This argument can apply to some, but not many, organization studies. The majority of organization studies have a managerial tilt, and this represents yet another complication. Our 'voices from the field' are completely literate, and in more or less the same language; in fact, my 'representations' are often in competition with theirs. Do we silence them by speaking for them? Do we represent them more fully than anybody else, considering that the 'otherness' is minimal? In his corporate ethnography Kunda (1992) portrayed a woman who taught 'organizational culture' in a corporation he was studying, and who had earlier obtained a Ph.D. in anthropology with a dissertation on this very subject. Who *was* he when studying her—'his sister's keeper' or a *doppelgänger*?

Two interesting glosses on that topic came from the field of the sociology of science and technology. Ashmore *et al.* (1989) took up the matter of political representation by interrogating a voice from the field, a 'Mrs Jones', who had this to say about sociologists' polyphonic ambitions:

---

[3] 'Voice' is a metaphor that has replaced 'perspective' in ethnographic parlance, in an act of rebellion against the visual, structuralist tone of the latter (see e.g. George Marcus, 1992).

[4] This reasoning is borrowed from Czarniawska (1997).

'I'm no more than a textual device of their making. I'm entirely under their control . . . I'm an illusion of multivocality . . . behind which the [social scientists] continue to assume their own privileged knowledge of the social world. So I think we need one more paradox: that social scientists can only claim to speak on our behalf by refusing to let us speak for ourselves. I think we'll call this the "paradox of applied social science".' (p. 208).

Within the narrative approach, there is something that is not a solution but a justification of the 'paradox of applied social science'. 'Mrs Jones' is indeed a textual device. This device has a long and honorable tradition in the novel. It is worth recalling that Tyler and Marcus took inspiration from Bakhtin when they spoke of their polyphony. And Bakhtin had in mind not a polyphony in which many people are speaking, but something called *heteroglossia*—that is 'variegated speech' or, in Russian, *raznorechje*. This is an authorial strategy consisting of the fact that the *author speaks different languages* (dialects, slangs, etc.) in the text. There is no need for the illusion that 'these people' talk for themselves; indeed they do not. But the author pays them a compliment by making the reader clearly aware of the fact that there *are* different languages being spoken within one and the same linguistic tradition, making the Otherness of the Other clear.

From this perspective it is easier to approach another suggestion coming from the sociology of science and technology: of meeting the duty of representation by giving voice even to non-humans (Callon 1986; Latour 1992*a*,*b*; 1993; Woolgar 1988). Latour (1996) put this suggestion in action in his study, which I discussed before, where Aramis got a voice of (his?) own. At a certain point in this story, Master and Pupil have a heated exchange on the sensibility of such a move: 'Do you think I don't know', barks the Master at the doubting Pupil, 'that giving Aramis a voice is but an anthropomorphization, creating a puppet with a voice? But if you think that puppets are "just ordinary things in our hands", then you've never talked to puppeteers' (p. 59).

In Bakhtinian terms, the author of *Aramis* uses variegated speech, which says a lot about his authorial talents, although he does not achieve symmetry between humans and non-humans, which is his aim. If anything, he magnifies the asymmetry. The reader does believe (unjustly so) that Mayor Chirac owns a voice, but not for even a moment that Aramis does.

When visiting La Villette (the Museum of Science and Industry in Paris), I became enchanted with a robot who introduced the visitors (especially children) to the museum. The robot walked (rolled), danced a bit, exchanged greetings in five languages, flashed its lamps, and allowed itself to be photographed with young visitors. Not wanting to be in the way of delighted children, I backed away from the robot until I bumped into somebody. Distracted from the spectacle by my clumsiness, I turned to apologize to the young man whom I had bumped into, only to realize that the robot's voice came from the same direction. Although he quickly vanished in the small crowd behind the robot, I could now see the remote controls in his pocket, and his lips barely moving to the hidden microphone as he greeted the next visitor. Another unemployed actor, no doubt.

We can become at best the spokespersons for others, *translating* their speech by saying something that we think they mean (as in the case of Mrs Jones or, for that matter, Aramis). In spite of centripetal forces at work, voices are irreducible to one another, and only translation is possible: but translation as a linguistic innovation, not as the 'same-saying' (MacIntyre 1988).

Thus we end up with a staged conversation in which the goal of political representation must live side by side with the awareness that we are performing an act of ventriloquism. This amounts to giving up the ambition of speaking on behalf of the Other in any literal sense, the ambition to be 'a tribune for the unheard, a representer of the unseen, a kenner of the misconstrued' (Geertz 1988: 133). In response to Mrs Jones's critique, and in defence of the Master, one can point out that, as any iconic representation or representations tested by correspondence are impossible, all that remains is political representation, often unasked for, always faulty by displacement, and always fictive. It might be suggested that the fictiveness of our polyphony, once revealed, relieves us from the criticism of silencing the voices. We do most harm when we impose our interpretations on what we claim are 'authentic voices from the field'. If rendering these voices to a wide audience is our goal, the way to go about it is to silence our own voices and to engage in the political activity of creating speaking platforms for those who are not heard.

Once it is clear to both authors and readers that our dialog is fictive, we can go further and admit that it can never be a democratic dialog on equal grounds. The author always has an initial advantage over the 'other' voices; the centripetal moves are the authorial device. But this does not mean that we cannot make centrifugal moves, even to the point of quarrelling with these voices if necessary: glossing over paradoxes, otherness, and conflict serves no one. Nor does it mean that the author always wins: a reader might decide otherwise, handing the laurel to the author's creation. Is, however, any communication possible in such a Babel Tower?

BABEL TOWER OR STANDARD ENGLISH?

The Genesis (11: 1–9) story of Babel Tower is, in brief, a story of polyphony, and the resulting crisis of meaning, as God's punishment. In the beginning, all people spoke one language, which was the language that God gave them, where, to put it in secular terms, each word had its precise referent. The Babylonians, however, sinned against God and wanted to make a name for themselves by building a tower whose top would reach heaven. God disrupted the work by so confusing the language of the workers that they could no longer understand each other. Since then people have been searching for that lost language. One should differentiate, however, between a *perfect language*—that which truly mirrors the nature of the world—and a *universal* language, which might be imperfect, but can be spoken by everybody (Eco 1995: 73). The language of the Babel Tower builders might have been both perfect and universal; since then, however, ambitions have been lowered, or, should one say, a division of labour has taken place. While the linguists look for a universal language, scientists look for a perfect one.[5]

Management and organization theory has a peculiar role in this enterprise. While admiring the ideals of science in the search for a perfect language, the management sciences have resigned themselves to the search for a universal one. Our legitimacy, as traditionally given, is to tell the truly universal story of organizing; to the extent that 'the managerialese' can be seen as a new Latin (Engwall 1992), our task is linguistic rather than scientific. This might reflect the ambiguity of the place business schools are given in universities. As posts in academia, they should be aspiring to find the truth, accessible perhaps only to a chosen few; as sites of practical education, they should form a language that everybody could adopt as their own. Nevertheless, a demand for polyphony is threatening to both those tasks.

Eco, in his historical report on the search for a perfect language, pointed out that, doomed to futility as the effort was, it did bring about a host of 'side effects', or as we call them, unintended consequences. The search for the perfect language gave birth to comparative linguistics, which, in turn, gave birth to the idea of a prototypical language (the Indo-European), which in turn gave rise to the idea of Aryan superiority, which in turn . . . Side effects are never uniformly positive or negative. Fiction writers have pursued this theme even further.

In Auster's *City of Glass*, a mad scientist, Stillman, tries to redo the experiment made many a time before, that of isolating a child from the world in the hope of rediscovering the prelapsarian language, where names stand firmly in a one-to-one relationship with things. It is the task of the New World, Stillman believes, to recreate this lost, Edenic state of affairs. He inscribes the words 'the tower of Babel' by his walks around New York, and collects objects that do not have proper names in order to give them names and improve the language. Quinn, a detective-story writer, turns detective, as, after all, there is no difference between the two: 'The detective is the one who looks, who listens, who moves through this morass of objects and events in search of the thought, the idea that will pull all these things together and make sense of them. In effect, the writer and the detective are interchangeable' (Auster 1989: 8). Thus Quinn tries to makes sense of Stillman's lunacy by writing down all that Stillman does, but when Stillman exits into suicide Quinn is left with no clues and he himself vanishes when his red notebook ends. One interpretation is, therefore, that, much as Stillman is a madman looking for perfect coincidence between words and things, so is every writer who tries to get events and words to fit.

In Ann S. Byatt's *Babel Tower* a manuscript appears called 'Babbletower', which is taken to court on the charge of obscenity (the prosecutor's name is Sir

---

[5]   In between there is the idea that a universal language is perfect not in the sense of mirroring the world, but the in constructions of the (universal) human mind—an idea that goes back to Plato.

Augustine). The witnesses for the defence consider the book to be 'a satirical work about the follies of utopian projectors' (Byatt 1996: 530) and set as its predecessors Fourier's *Nouveau Monde Amoureux* and Sade's *Château de Silling*. This last opinion, offered by a woman professor of French literature, summarizes neatly the manuscript, which tells the story of Utopia as a sado-erotic enterprise, where women and children become the first victims.

This reading made me notice that the story of the search for the perfect language, as told in historical detail by Eco, is a story with male characters only. The search for the perfect language seems to be a man's folly, and it drags women into it on dangerous conditions. As Auster retells it (via Stillman's manuscript), 'the building of the Tower became the obsessive overriding passion of mankind, more important finally than life itself. Bricks became more precious than people. Women laborers did not even stop to give birth to their children; they secured the new born in their aprons and went right on working' (1989: 44).

Neal Stephenson's *Snow Crash* reads the story of Babel Tower from the cybertime/space point of view and interprets it as an introduction of a neuro-logical virus, or rather countervirus, which destroyed the mental unity of its builders (caused by the metavirus, or Creation), thereby saving humanity from being open to totalitarian programming achievable via a common language. 'Maybe Babel was the best thing that ever happened to us', concludes one of the characters (Stephenson 1993: 279). Babel, that is, the Gate of God, 'is a gateway in our minds, a gateway that was opened by the [countervirus] that broke us free from the metavirus and gave us the ability to think—moved us from a materialistic world to a dualistic world—a binary world—with both a physical and a spiritual component' (p. 388). Snow crash is a new virus, a new drug, a new program that aims at reverting this incident and turning people into a crowd of blah-blahing infants, skillfully controlled by a Pentecostal sect who released the virus. Leaving aside the question whether we are content with a binary, dualist world, Stephenson's reading is similar to that of Byatt: the dream of a perfect language is a totalitarian night-mare. And the name of the electronic library one of the protagonists uses is: 'Babel/Infocalypse'.

Eco himself (1995) lists another deviant interpretation of the Babel Tower: not as a wound in the common fate of humanity but, in the reading of Luther, as a fantastic technological achievement of the humans. In the same vein, Dante suggested that the linguistic conflict was, in fact, a professional or occupational conflict: something like when, nowadays, the accounting department finds it difficult to talk to marketing. In that sense, the social divi-sion of labor is actually a social linguistic division; each corporation is a Babel Tower. And, if George Steiner is right, this 'prodigality of diverse languages' (1975/1992: p. xv) has a strong survival value. It may present a problem to orga-nization scholars, but hardly to humankind. The scholars must then find the best ways of tackling of this obstacle, and there are many attempts to do just that.

LIFE IN THE BAZAAR

Eco observed that, at least within philosophy, some learning can be claimed to have happened: 'The dream had changed, or, perhaps, its limitations had finally, reluctantly been accepted. From its search for the lost language of Adam, philosophy had by now learned to take only what it could get' (1995: 313). And that is not a perfect language, but possibly, a universal language; not *a priori*, but *a posteriori*, not found but created. In principle, everyone can learn BASIC or FORTRAN, but hardly anybody would claim their superiority to natural languages.

In relation to natural languages, there is no way out but acceptance of polyphony (Steiner 1992). As to the remaining two ways, one is unrealistic and the other is unacceptable. The first is to compare information of every possible language that exists or existed: possible in principle, unrealizable in practice. The second is to deduce the universal structure of the human mind from one natural language—which, as it usually happens, is the analyst's own language. In this way one natural language is promoted to a metalanguage and the analysis is prejudiced from the start, which brings us to the political issue, that of globalized (translocal) versus local languages. A language may become universal by virtue of politics, not by virtue of its closeness to the structure of the human mind.

Social sciences underwent a parallel self-reflection. This effort produced, on the one hand, a plethora of renewed pleas for a concerted search for the perfect and/or universal language; on the other hand, a recommendation to enjoy the polyvocal noise of postmodernity. And yet this dichotomy may be misleading. The thesis that 'there is no single commensurating language, known in advance, that will provide an idiom into which to translate any new theory, poetic idiom, or native culture' is not the same as the thesis that 'there are unlearnable languages' (Rorty 1992*a*: 64).

In their recent book, Berger and Luckmann (1995) pointed out that the 'search for perfect language' can be equaled with fundamentalism. A society, or a group within a society, clings to and attempts to glorify 'one set of values "imported" from the stocks of the musée imaginaire of meanings' (p. 25). Not only the museum is imaginary, as pointed out by many scholars observing the 'reinvention of traditions', but it is likely that there are many such sets imported at the same time. The result is exactly what was to be avoided: a modern pluralism, which, through a thorough relativization of systems of values and schemes of interpretation, 'decanonizes' them (pp. 38–9). Berger and Luckmann's stance is as follows:[6]

---

[6] I ought to remind the reader at this point that Berger and Luckmann's (1995) stance is influenced by their adoption of Diltheyan dichotomy of 'nature' and 'culture', 'explanation' and 'understanding'. Rorty (1991*a*), among others, shows convincingly why these dichotomies cannot be retained.

Between the impossibility of the 'relativistic' reaction to modernity and the frightening possibilities of 'fundamentalism', there is another position. As best one can, one reconciles oneself to the negative consequences of structural differentiation and modern pluralism. One opposes the danger of the destruction of modern society by totalitarian regression, but sees no reason to join in the celebration of modern pluralism. . . . This unspectacular but by no means passive basic position also has implications for media policy—way beyond the social and cultural policies of the state. It is the responsibility of the leaders of the agencies communicating meaning, e.g. the mass media, to support intermediary institutions within the context of a deregulated market in meaning. (p. 63)

To convince these leaders to adopt such a stance is, I imagine, the responsibility of social scientists. Berger and Luckmann also manage to diminish the supposedly catastrophic proportions of the crisis of meaning caused by plurality by pointing out that, 'whereas life-communities must presume a minimum community of meaning, the inverse is not true. Communities of meaning may under certain circumstances become communities of life, they may however be built up and maintained exclusively through mediated, reciprocal action' (p. 22). This gets us, social scientists, off the hook, and leaves the practitioners half-hanging. The Tower of Babel was, after all, an organizational enterprise. Having lost their common language, the builders of the Tower could not accomplish their task but they continued to live dispersed all over the world. Indeed, the builders of La Tour Bruyarde in Ann Byatt's novel were endangered by this enterprise only as long as they were a community of life. Had they managed to escape, they could live happily and even—the worst wounds healed—remain 'a Babel Tower community of meaning'. This is also a reading proffered by Kaghan and Phillips (1998), who saw the Babel Tower as a community of practice.

This leads, in my view, to an interesting paradox of organizational practice. In order to continue building any towers at all, the practitioners must continue their (hopeless) search for the perfect language. The more they succeed, however, the bigger the chance that the repeated confrontations with plurality waiting outside the organization's door will have strongly traumatic, not to say existentially threatening influence on their members. I pointed this out in my work on ideological control (Czarniawska-Joerges 1988), and it has been powerfully restated by, for example, Kunda (1992) and the contributors to Fineman's (1993) collection of papers on emotions in organizations. The horrible community of Byatt's La Tour Bruyarde was destroying itself in step with their success.

Although Berger and Luckmann are offering what can at best be called a liberal gloss on a basically statist conception of polity, their stress on intermediary institutions (that is, those mediating between the individual, or the family and the state) places them close to Alasdair MacIntyre's more radical communitarianism, in which he would like to see intermediary institutions replacing the state. The liberalist state, he claims, has failed to take up issues central to contemporary societies; among others, the issue of plurality. He sets up another position in between fundamentalism and relativism, in the vicinity of the latter, the perspectivist stance:

The relativist challenge rests upon a denial that rational debate between and rational choice among rival traditions is possible; the perspectivist challenge puts in question the possibility of making truth-claims from within any one tradition. For if there is a multiplicity of rival traditions, each with its own characteristic modes of rational justifications internal to it, then that very fact entails that no one tradition can offer those outside it good reasons for excluding the theses of its rivals. What seemed to require rival traditions so to exclude and so to deny was belief in the logical incompatibility of the theses asserted and denied within rival traditions, a belief which embodied a recognition that if the theses of one such tradition were true, then some at least of the theses asserted by its rivals were false.

  The solution, so the perspectivist argues, is to withdraw the ascription of truth and falsity, at least in the sense in which 'true' and 'false' have been understood so far within the practice of such traditions, both from individual theses and from the bodies of systematic belief of which such theses are constitutive parts. Instead of interpreting rival traditions as mutually exclusive and incompatible ways of understanding one and the same world, one and the same subject matter, let us understand them instead as providing very different, complementary perspectives for envisaging the realities about which they speak to us.   (MacIntyre 1988: 352)

I believe that this solution could be directly applied to organization studies. Instead of adjudicating between different truth claims (management or workers? marketing department or accounting department?), we can present them as explicable from their perspective; next, we can show how they are translated into collective action. This I perceive to be a legitimate—if demanding—task facing our discipline: to show how all those people speaking incompatible languages accomplish so much together.

  Berger and Luckmann conceptualized a contemporary society as an open market for meanings, which makes us—organization researchers—into merchants of meaning together with, let us say, consultants and journalists. Rorty (1991*b*) radicalized this picture further by speaking about a bazaar, a far cry from the elegant 'free market' where the demand neatly and silently controls the supply. There is a lot of noise and haggling in the bazaar. Suggesting a 'consolidation' of the discipline amounts to a proposal that we should attempt to offer our product as monolingual. At a bazaar where our potential 'buyers' speak more languages and dialects than we could ever master?

  Management and organization studies confront a world that is, and will remain, polyphonic and polysemic. The uneasy task of organization scholars is to render this state of affairs in our texts, which requires a skillful balance between centripetal and centrifugal textual moves.

REFERENCES

AGGER, BEN (1990), *The Decline of Discourse: Reading, Writing and Resistance in Postmodern Capitalism* (New York: Falmer Press).

ALEXANDERSSON, OLA, and TROSSMARK, PER (1997), *Konstruktion av förnyelse i organisationer* (Lund: Lund University Press).

ALVESSON, MATS (1993), 'Organization as Rhetoric; Ambiguity in Knowledge-Intensive Companies', *Journal of Management Studies*, 30/6: 997–1015.

—— and WILLMOTT, HUGH (1992) (eds.), *Critical Management Studies* (London: Sage).

ARGYRIS, CHRIS, and SCHÖN, DONALD (1974), *Theory in Practice: Increasing Professional Effectiveness* (San Francisco: Jossey-Bass).

ARNOLD, THURMAN W. (1935), *The Symbols of Government* (New Haven: Yale University Press).

ASHMORE, MALCOLM (1989), *The Reflexive Thesis: Wrighting Sociology of Scientific Knowledge* (Chicago: University of Chicago Press).

—— MULKAY, MICHAEL, and PINCH, TREVOR (1989), *Health Efficiency: A Sociology of Health Economics* (Milton Keynes: Open University Press).

ASTLEY, GRAHAM W., and ZAMMUTO, RAYMOND F. (1992), 'Organization Science, Managers, and Language Games', *Organization Science*, 3/4: 443–60.

AUSTER, PAUL (1989), 'City of Glass', in *The New York Trilogy* (London: Faber & Faber).

BAKHTIN, MICHAIL M. (1981), 'Discourse in the Novel', in *The Dialogic Imagination. Four Essays* (Austin, Tex.: University of Texas Press), 259–422.

——/MEDVEDEV, PAVEL N. (1928/1985), *The Formal Method in Literary Scholarship: A Crititical Introduction to Sociological Poetics* (Cambridge, Mass.: Harvard University Press).

—— —— (1928/1994), 'Literature as Ideological Form', in Pam Morris (ed.), *The Bakhtin Reader* (London: Edward Arnold), 123–34.

BARNARD, CHESTER I. (1938), *The Functions of the Executive* (Cambridge, Mass.: Harvard University Press).

BARRY, DAVID, and ELMES, MICHAEL (1997), 'Strategy Retold: Toward a Narrative View of Strategic Discourse', *Academy of Management Review*, 22/2: 429–52.

BAUMAN, ZYGMUNT (1992), *Intimations of Postmodernity* (London: Routledge).

BERGER, PETER, and LUCKMANN, THOMAS (1966), *The Social Construction of Reality* (New York: Doubleday).

—— —— (1995), *Modernity, Pluralism and the Crisis of Meaning* (Gütersloh: Bertelsmann Foundation Publishers).

BERNSTEIN, J. M. (1990), 'Self-Knowledge as Praxis: Narrative and Narration in

Psychoanalysis', in Cristopher Nash (ed.), *Narrative in Culture: The Uses of Storytelling in the Sciences, Philosophy and Literature* (London: Routledge), 51–77.

BHASKAR, ROY (1989), *Reclaiming Reality: A Critical Introduction to Contemporary Philosophy* (London: Verso).

BODEN, DEIRDRE (1994), *The Business of Talk: Organizations in Action* (Cambridge: Polity Press).

—— and ZIMMERMAN, DON H. (1991) (eds.), *Talk and Social Structure* (Cambridge: Polity Press).

BOJE, DAVID (1991), 'The Story-Telling Organization: A Study of Story Performance in an Office-Supply Firm', *Administrative Science Quarterly*, 36: 106–26.

BOLAND, RICHARD J., JR. (1989), 'Beyond the Objectivist and the Subjectivist: Learning to Read Accounting as Text', *Accounting, Organizations and Society*, 14/5–6: 591–604.

—— (1994), 'Identity, Economy and Morality in *The Rise of Silas Lapham*', in Barbara Czarniawska-Joerges and Pierre Guillet de Monthoux (eds.), *Good Novels, Better Management* (Reading: Harwood Academic Publishers), 115–37.

—— and TANKASI, RAMKRISHNAN V. (1995), 'Perspective Making and Perspective Taking in Communities of Knowing', *Organization Science*, 6/3: 350–72.

BONFANTINI, MASSIMO A., and PRONI, GIAMPAOLO (1983), 'To Guess or Not to Guess?', in Umberto Eco and Thomas A. Sebeok (eds.), *Il segno dei tre: Holmes, Dupin, Peirce* (Milano: Bompianti), 139–55.

BOURDIEU, PIERRE (1977), *The Outline of a Theory of Practice* (Cambridge: Cambridge University Press).

BOYD, WILLIAM (1998), *Armadillo* (London: Hamish Hamilton).

BRADBURY, MALCOLM (1992), 'Closer to Chaos: American Fiction in the 1980s', *Times Literary Supplement*, 22: 17.

BROWN, RICHARD H. (1977), *A Poetic for Sociology: Toward a Logic of Discovery for the Human Sciences* (New York: Cambridge University Press).

—— (1980), 'The Position of Narrative in Contemporary Society', *New Literary History*, 11/3: 545–50.

—— (1987), *Society as Text: Essays on Rhetoric, Reason and Reality* (Chicago: University of Chicago Press).

—— (1989), *Social Science as Civic Discourse: Essays on the Invention, Legitimation and Uses of Social Theory* (Chicago: University of Chicago Press).

BRUNER, JEROME (1986), *Actual Minds, Possible Worlds* (Cambridge, Mass.: Harvard University Press).

—— (1990), *Acts of Meaning* (Cambridge, Mass.: Harvard University Press).

BRUNSSON, NILS (1982), *Företagsekonomi: språk eller moral?* (Lund: Studentlitteratur).

—— (1985), *The Irrational Organization* (London: Wiley).

—— (1989), *The Organization of Hypocrisy: Talk, Decision and Actions in Organizations* (Chichester: Wiley).

—— and OLSEN, JOHAN (1993) (eds.), *The Reforming Organization* (London: Routledge).

BRUSS, ELISABETH W. (1976), *Autobiographical Acts: The Changing Situation of a Literary Genre* (Baltimore: Johns Hopkins University Press).

—— (1982), *Beautiful Theories* (Baltimore: Johns Hopkins University Press).

BURAWOY, MICHAEL (1979), *Manufacturing Consent* (Chicago: University of Chicago Press).

BURKE, KENNETH (1945/1969), *A Grammar of Motives* (Berkeley and Los Angeles: University of California Press).

BURRELL, GIBSON, and MORGAN, GARETH (1979), *Sociological Paradigms and Organizational Analysis* (Aldershot: Gower).

——— REED, MICHAEL, CALÁS, MARTA, SMIRCICH, LINDA, and ALVESSON, MATS (1994), 'Why Organization? Why Now?', *Organization*, 1/1: 5–17.

BYATT, ANN S. (1996), *Babel Tower* (London: Chatto & Windus).

CALÁS, MARTA, and SMIRCICH, LINDA (1991), 'Voicing Seduction to Silence Leadership', *Organization Studies*, 12/4: 567–601.

——— ——— (1993) (eds.), *Unbounding Organizational Analysis: Questioning 'Globalization' Through Third World Women's Voices* (Academy of Management Meeting Symposium, Atlanta, 10 Aug.).

CALLON, MICHEL (1986), 'Some Elements of a Sociology of Translation: Domestication of the Scallops and the Fishermen of St Brieuc's Bay', in John Law (ed.), *Power, Action and Belief* (London: Routledge & Kegan Paul), 196–229.

CAPPETTI, CARLA (1995), *Writing Chicago. Modernism, Ethnography and the Novel* (New York: Columbia University Press).

CARSANIGA, GIOVANNI M. (1978), 'Realism in Italy', in Fredrick W. J. Hemmings (ed.), *The Age of Realism* (Sussex: Harvester Press), 323–55.

CASTANEDA, CARLOS (1968/1986), *The Teachings of Don Juan: A Yaqui Way of Knowledge* (Harmondsworth: Penguin).

CHANDLER, RAYMOND (1950), 'The Simple Art of Murder', in *Pearls Are a Nuisance* (London: Penguin), 181–99.

CLARK, BURTON R. (1972), 'The Organizational Saga in Higher Education', *Administrative Science Quarterly*, 17: 178–84.

CLIFFORD, JAMES, and MARCUS, GEORGE E. (1986) (eds.), *Writing Culture: The Poetics and Politics of Ethnography* (Berkeley and Los Angeles: University of California Press).

COHEN, MICHAEL D., MARCH, JAMES G., and OLSEN, JOHAN (1972), 'A Garbage Can Model of Organizational Choice', *Administrative Science Quarterly*, 17/1 (1972); repr. in James G. March, *Decisions and Organizations* (Oxford: Blackwell), 294–334.

CZARNIAWSKA-JOERGES, BARBARA (1988), *Ideological Control in Non-Ideological Organizations* (New York: Praeger).

——— (1989), *Economic Decline and Organizational Control* (New York: Praeger).

——— (1994), 'Gender, Power, Organizations: An Interruptive Interpretation', in John Hassard and Martin Parker (eds.), *Towards a New Theory of Organizations* (London: Routledge), 227–47.

CZARNIAWSKA, BARBARA (1996), 'The Process of Organizing', in *International Encyclopaedia of Business and Management* (London: Routledge), 3966–81.

——— (1997), *Narrating the Organization: Dramas of Institutional Identity* (Chicago: University of Chicago Press).

——— (1998), *A Narrative Approach in Organization Studies* (Thousand Oaks, Calif.: Sage).

CZARNIAWSKA-JOERGES, BARBARA, and GUILLET DE MONTHOUX, PIERRE (1994) (eds.), *Good Novels, Better Management: Reading Realities in Fiction* (Reading: Harwood Academic Press).

CZARNIAWSKA, BARBARA, and JOERGES, BERNWARD (1995), 'Winds of Organizational Change: How Ideas Translate Into Objects and Actions', in Samuel Bacharach, Pasquale Gagliardi, and Brian Mundell (eds.), *Studies of Organizations in the European Tradition* (Greenwich, Conn.: JAI Press), 171–209.

——— and SEVÓN, GUJE (1996) (eds.), *Translating Organizational Change* (Berlin: de Gruyter).

D'ORMESSON, JEAN (1971), *La Gloire de l'Empire* (Paris: Gallimard).

DALTON, MELVILLE (1959), *Men Who Manage: Fusions of Feeling and Theory in Administration* (New York: Wiley).

DAVIES, BRONWYN (1989), *Frogs and Snails and Feminist Tales* (North Sydney: Allen & Unwin).

DEMOTT, BENJAMIN (1989), 'Reading Fiction to the Bottom Line', *Harvard Business Review* (May–June), 128–34.

DIPPLE, ELISABETH (1970), *Plot* (London: Methuen).

DOUGLAS, MARY (1986), *How Institutions Think* (London: Routledge & Kegan Paul).

DOYLE, ARTHUR CONAN (1981), *The Penguin Complete Sherlock Holmes* (London: Penguin).

DURKHEIM, ÉMILE, and MAUSS, MARCEL (1903/1963), *Primitive Classifications* (London: Cohen & West).

ECO, UMBERTO (1979/1983), *The Role of the Reader: Explorations in the Semiotics of Texts* (London: Hutchinson).

—— (1990), *The Limits of Interpretation* (Bloomington, Ind.: Indiana University Press).

—— (1992), *Interpretation and Overinterpretation* (Cambridge: Cambridge University Press).

—— (1995), *In Search for the Perfect Language* (Oxford: Blackwell).

—— and SEBEOK, THOMAS A. (1983) (eds.), *Il segno dei tre: Holmes, Dupin, Peirce* (Milano: Bompianti).

Encyclopaedia Britannica (1989), Micropaedia.

ENGWALL, LARS (1992), *Mercury Meets Minerva* (Oxford: Pergamon Press).

FAY, BRIAN (1990), '*Critical* Realism?', *Journal for the Theory of Social Behaviour*, 20/1: 33–41.

FELDMAN, MARTHA (1995), *Strategies for Interpreting Qualitative Data* (Newbury Park, Calif.: Sage.

FEYERABEND, PAUL (1957/1988), *Against Method* (London: Verso).

FINEMAN, STEPHEN (1993) (ed.), *Emotion in Organizations* (London: Sage).

FISHER, WALTER R. (1984), 'Narration as a Human Communication Paradigm: The Case of Public Moral Argument', *Communication Monographs*, 51: 1–22.

—— (1987), *Human Communication as Narration: Toward a Philosophy of Reason, Value, and Action* (Columbia, SC: University of South Carolina Press).

FOKKEMA, DOUWE W. (1984), *Literary History, Modernism and Postmodernism* (Amsterdam: John Benjamins).

FORESTER, JOHN (1992), 'Critical Ethnography: On Fieldwork in a Habermasian Way', in Mats Alvesson and Hugh Willmott (eds.), *Critical Management Studies* (London: Sage), 46–65.

FREEBORN, R. H. (1978), 'Realism in Russia, to the Death of Dostoyevsky', in Fredrick W. J. Hemmings (ed.), *The Age of Realism* (Sussex: Harvester Press), 69–141.

FRIEDMAN, MILTON (1953), *Essays in Positive Economics* (Chicago: University of Chicago Press).

FROST, PETER J., MITCHELL, V. F., and NORD, WALTER S. (1978), *Organizational Reality: Reports from the Firing Line* (Santa Monica, Calif.: Goodyear).

—— MOORE, LARRY F., LOUIS, MERYL REIS, LUNDBERG, CRAIG C., and MARTIN, JOANNE (1985) (eds.), *Organizational Culture* (Newbury Park, Calif.: Sage).

—— —— —— —— —— (1991) (eds.), *Reframing Organizational Culture* (Newbury Park, Calif.: Sage).

FRYE, NORTHROP (1957/1990), *The Anatomy of Criticism* (London: Penguin).

—— (1973), 'The Social Context of Literary Criticism', in Elisabeth and Thomas Burns (eds.), *Sociology of Literature and Drama* (Harmondsworth: Penguin), 138–58.

GABRIEL, YIANNIS (1995), 'The Unmanaged Organization: Stories, Fantasies and Subjectivity', *Organization Studies*, 16/3: 477–502.

GAGLIARDI, PASQUALE (1990) (ed.), *The Symbolics of the Artifacts* (Berlin: de Gruyter).

GEERTZ, CLIFFORD (1973), *The Interpretation of Cultures* (New York: Basic Books).

—— (1988), *Works and Lives: The Anthropologist as Author* (Stanford: Stanford University Press).

GHERARDI, SILVIA (1994), 'The Gender We Think, the Gender We Do in our Everyday Organizational Lives', *Human Relations*, 47/6: 591–610.

GIDDENS, ANTHONY (1990), *The Consequences of Modernity* (Cambridge: Polity Press).

—— (1991), *Modernity and Self-Identity: Self and Society in the Late Modern Age* (Cambridge: Polity Press).

GINZBURG, CARLO (1983), 'Spie: Radici di un paradigma indiziario', in Umberto Eco and Thomas A. Sebeok (eds.), *Il segno dei tre: Holmes, Dupin, Peirce* (Milan: Bompianti), 95–136.

GLASER, BARNEY, and STRAUSS, ANSELM (1967), *The Discovery of Grounded Theory* (Chicago: Aldine).

GOFFMAN, ERVING (1981), *Forms of Talk* (Oxford: Basil Blackwell).

GOLDEN-BIDDLE, KAREN, and LOCKE, KAREN (1993), 'Appealing Work: An Investigation of How Ethnographic Texts Convince', *Organization Science*, 4/4: 595–616.

—— (1997), *Composing Qualitative Research* (Thousand Oaks, Calif.: Sage).

GOODALL, H. L., Jr. (1994), *Casing a Promised Land: The Autobiography of an Organizational Detective as Cultural Ethnographer* (Carbondale. Ill.: Southern Illinois University Press).

—— (1978), *Ways of Worldmaking* (Indianapolis: Hackett).

—— (1984), *Of Mind and Other Matters* (Cambridge, Mass.: Harvard University Press).

GOODY, JACK (1986),*The Logic of Writing and the Organization of Society* (Cambridge: Cambridge University Press).

—— and WATT, IAN (1968), 'The Consequences of Literacy', in Jack Goody (ed.), *Literacy in Traditional Societies* (Cambridge: Cambridge University Press), 27–68.

GOULDNER, ALVIN (1954), *Patterns of Industrial Bureaucracy* (Glencoe, Ill.: Free Press).

GUBA, EDWIN G. (1981), 'Criteria for Assessing Truthworthiness of Naturalistic Inquiries', *Educational Communication and Technology Journal*, 29/2: 75–91.

—— (1985), 'The Context of Emergent Paradigm Research', in Yvonne S. Lincoln (ed.), *Organizational Theory and Inquiry: The Paradigm Revolution* (Beverly Hills, Calif.: Sage).

HARRÉ, ROM (1986),*Varieties of Realism* (Oxford: Basil Blackwell).

HATCH, MARY JO (1996), 'The Role of the Researcher: An Analysis of Narrative Position in Organization Theory', *Journal of Management Inquiry*, 5/4: 359–74.

HEMMINGS, FREDRICK W. J. (1978*a*), 'Realism and the Novel: The Eighteenth-Century Beginnings', in Fredrick W. J. Hemmings (ed.), *The Age of Realism* (Brighton: Harvester Press), 3–35.

—— (1978*b*), 'The Decline of Realism', in Fredrick W. J. Hemmings (ed.), *The Age of Realism* (Brighton: Harvester Press), 323–40.

HERNADI, PAUL (1987), 'Literary Interpretation and the Rhetoric of the Human Sciences', in John S. Nelson, Allan Megill, and D. N. McCloskey (eds.), *The Rhetoric of the Human Sciences* (Wisconsin, Md.: University of Wisconsin Press), 263–75.

HIRSCHMAN, ALBERT O. (1977), *Exit, Voice, Loyalty* (Cambridge, Mass.: Harvard University Press).

HOLZNER, BURKHARD (1968), *Reality Construction in Society* (Cambridge, Mass.: Schenkman).

HORTON, RICHARD (1996), 'Truth and Heresy about AIDS', *New York Review of Books*, 23 May: 14–20.

HOSKINS, KEITH (1996), A seminar at London School of Economics, 5 Mar.

HÖPFL, HEATHER (1995), 'Organizational Rhetoric and the Threat of Ambivalence', *Studies in Cultures, Organizations and Societies*, 1/2: 175–88.

HÜHN, PETER (1987), 'The Detective as Reader: Narrativity and Reading Concepts in Detective Fiction', *Modern Fiction Studies*, 33/3: 451–66.

IRIGARAY, LUCE (1985), *This Sex which is not One* (Ithaca, NY: Cornell University Press).

ISAAC, J. C. (1990), 'Realism and Reality: Some Realistic Considerations', *Journal for the Theory of Social Behaviour*, 20/1: 1–31.

ISER, WOLFGANG (1978), *The Art of Reading: A Theory of Aesthetic Response* (Baltimore, Md.: Johns Hopkins University Press).

JANION, MARIA (1996), *Kobiety i duch innosci* (Warsaw: Wydawnictwo Sic!).

JAQUES, ELLIOT (1951), *The Changing Culture of a Factory* (London: Tavistock).

KAGHAN, WILLIAM, and PHILLIPS, NELSON (1998), 'Building the Tower of Babel: Communities of Practice and Paradigmatic Pluralism in Organization Studies', *Organization*, 5/2: 191–215.

KNORR CETINA, KARIN (1981), *The Manufacture of Knowledge: An Essay on the Constructivist and Contextual Nature of Science* (Oxford: Pergamon).

—— (1994), 'Primitive Classification and Postmodernity: Towards a Sociological Notion of Fiction', *Theory, Culture & Society*, 11: 1–22.

KUHN, THOMAS (1964/1996), *The Structure of Scientific Revolutions* (Chicago: University of Chicago Press).

KUNDA, GIDEON (1992), *Engineering Culture: Control and Commitment in a High-Tech Organization* (Philadelphia: Temple University Press).

KUNDERA, MILAN (1988), *The Art of the Novel* (London: Faber & Faber).

LAMARQUE, PETER (1990), 'Narrative and Invention: The Limits of Fictionality', in Cristopher Nash (ed.), *Narrative in Culture: The Uses of Storytelling in the Sciences, Philosophy and Literature* (London: Routledge), 5–22.

LATOUR, BRUNO (1986), 'The Power of Associations', in John Law (ed.), *Power, Action and Belief* (London: Routledge & Kegan Paul), 261–77.

—— (1988a), 'The Politics of Explanation: An Alternative', in Steve Woolgar (ed.), *Knowledge and Reflexivity* (London: Sage), 155–77.

—— (1988b), 'A Relativistic Account of Einstein's Relativity', *Social Studies of Science*, 18: 3–44.

—— (1992a), 'The Next Turn After the Social Turn . . . ', in Ernan McMullin (ed.), *The Social Dimensions of Science* (Notre Dame, Ind.: University of Notre Dame Press), 272–92.

—— (1992b), 'Technology is Society Made Durable', in John Law (ed.), *A Sociology of Monsters: Essays on Power, Technology and Domination* (London: Routledge), 103–31.

—— (1993), *We Have Never Been Modern* (Cambridge, Mass.: Harvard University Press).

—— (1996), *Aramis or the Love of Technology* (Cambridge, Mass.: Harvard University Press).

LAW, JOHN (1994), *Organizing Modernity* (Oxford: Blackwell).

LEIDNER, ROBIN (1993), *Fast Food, Fast Talk: Service Work and the Routinization of Everyday Life* (Berkeley and Los Angeles: University of California Press).

LEJEUNE, PHILIPPE (1989), *On Autobiography* (Minneapolis: University of Minnesota Press).

LEPENIES, WOLF (1988), *Between Literature and Science: The Rise of Sociology* (Cambridge: Cambridge University Press).

LEVIN, HARRY (1973), 'Literature as an Institution', in Elisabeth and Tom Burns (eds.), *Sociology of Literature and Drama* (Harmondsworth: Penguin), 56–70.

LEVINE, GEORGE (1993), 'Looking for the Real: Epistemology in Science and Culture', in George Levine (ed.), *Realism and Representation: Essays on the Problem of Realism in Relation to Science, Literature, and Culture* (Madison: University of Wisconsin Press), 3–26.

LEWIN, KURT (1953), *Field Theory in Social Science* (New York: Harper).

—— LIPPIT, ROBERT, and WHITE, R. K. (1939), 'Patterns of Aggressive Behavior in Experimentally Created "Social Climates" ', *Journal of Social Psychology*, 10: 271–99.

LINCOLN, YVONNE S. (1985), 'The Substance of the Emergent Paradigm: Implications for Researchers', in Yvonne S. Lincoln (ed.), *Organizational Theory and Inquiry: The Paradigm Revolution* (Beverly Hills, Calif.: Sage), 137–57.

LUHMANN, NIKLAS (1991), 'Sthenographie und Euryalistik', in Hans Ulrich Gumbrecht and Karl-Ludwig Pfeiffer (eds.), *Paradoxien, Dissonanzen, Zusammenbrüche. Situationen offener Epistemologie* (Frankfurt: Suhrkamp), 58–82.

LYOTARD, JEAN-FRANÇOIS (1979/1987), *The Postmodern Condition: A Report on Knowledge* (Manchester: Manchester University Press).

McCLOSKEY, D. N. (1986), *The Rhetoric of Economics* (Wisconsin, Md.: University of Wisconsin Press).

—— (1990*a*), *If You're So Smart: The Narrative of Economic Expertise* (Wisconsin, Ma.: University of Wisconsin Press).

—— (1990*b*), 'Storytelling in Economics', in Cristopher Nash (ed.), *Narrative in Culture: The Uses of Storytelling in the Sciences, Philosophy and Literature* (London: Routledge), 5–22.

MacINTYRE, ALASDAIR (1981/1990), *After Virtue* (London: Duckworth Press).

—— (1988), *Whose Justice? Which Rationality?* (London: Duckworth Press).

MANICAS, PETER T., and ROSENBERG, ALAN (1988), 'Can We Ever Get It Right?', *Journal for the Theory of Social Behaviour*, 18/1: 51–76.

MANOUKIAN, FRANCA OLIVETTI (1994), 'Power, Time, Talk and Money: Organizations in Italian Literature', in Barbara Czarniawska-Joerges and Pierre Guillet de Monthoux (eds.), *Good Novels, Better Management: Reading Realities in Fiction* (Reading: Harwood Academic Press), 154–74.

MARCH, JAMES G., and OLSEN, JOHAN (1989), *Rediscovering Institutions: The Organizational Basis of Politics* (New York: Free Press).

—— and SIMON, HERBERT A. (1958/1993), *Organizations* (Oxford: Blackwell).

MARCUS, GEORGE E. (1992), 'Past, Present and Emergent Identities: Requirements for Ethnographies of Late Twentieth-Century Modernity Worldwide', in Scott Lash and Jonathan Friedman (eds.), *Modernity and Identity* (Oxford: Blackwell), 309–30.

—— and FISCHER, MICHAEL M. (1986), *Anthropology as Cultural Critique: An Experimental Moment in the Human Sciences* (Chicago: University of Chicago Press).

MARCUS, STEVEN (1974), 'Introduction' to Dashiell Hammett, *The Continental Op* (New York: Vintage Books), pp. vii–xxix.

MARTIN, JOANNE (1982), 'Stories and Scripts in Organizational Settings', in A. H. Hastrof and A. M. Isen (eds.), *Cognitive Social Psychology* (New York: North Holland-Elsevier), 165–94.

—— (1990), 'Deconstructing Organizational Taboos: The Suppression of Gender Conflict in Organizations', *Organization Science*, 1/4: 339–59.

—— FELDMAN, MARTHA, HATCH, MARY JO, and SITKIN, SIM B. (1983), 'The Uniqueness Paradox in Organizational Stories', *Administrative Science Quarterly*, 28: 438–53.

MELLING, JOHN KENNEDY (1996), *Murder Done to Death: Parody and Pastiche in Detective Fiction* (Lanham, Md.: Scarecrow Press).

MEYER, JOHN (1996), 'Otherhood: The Promulgation and Transmission of Ideas in the Modern Organizational Environment', in Barbara Czarniawska and Guje Sevón (eds.), *Translating Organizational Change* (Berlin: de Gruyter), 241–52.

MINTZBERG, HENRY (1991), 'A Letter to Marta Calás and Linda Smircich', *Organization Studies*, 12/4: 602.

MITCHELL, W. J. T. (1987), *Iconology* (Chicago: University of Chicago Press).

MITROFF, IAN, and KILMANN, RALPH (1975), 'Stories Managers Tell: A New Tool for Organizational Problem Solving', *Management Review*, 64: 13–28.

MORGAN, GARETH (1986), *Images of Organization* (London: Sage).

MULKAY, MICHAEL (1985), *The Word and the World: Explorations in the Form of Sociological Analysis* (London: George Allen & Unwin).

NELSON, JOHN S., MEGILL, ALLAN, and McCLOSKEY, D. N. (1987) (eds.), *The Rhetoric of the Human Sciences* (Wisconsin, Md.: University of Wisconsin Press).

NICOLSON, MARJORIE (1946), 'The Professor and the Detective', in Howard Haycraft (ed.), *The Art of the Mystery Story* (New York: Simon), 110–27.

OAKESHOTT, MICHAEL (1959/1991), 'The Voice of Poetry in the Conversation of Mankind', in *Rationalism in Politics and Other Essays* (Indianapolis: Liberty Press), 488–541.

O'CONNOR, ELLEN S. (1996), 'Lines of Authority: Readings of Foundational Texts on the Profession of Management', *Journal of Management History*, 2/3: 26–49.

—— (1997), 'Discourse at our Disposal: Stories in and around the Garbage Can', *Management Communication Quarterly*, 10/4: 395–432.

PARKER, ROBERT B. (1988), 'Introduction' to Dashiell Hammett, *Woman in the Dark* (New York: Vintage Books), pp. ix–xiv.

PASCALE, RICHARD T. (1984), 'Perspectives on Strategy: The Real Story behind Honda's Success', *California Management Review*, 26/3: 47–72.

PERROW, CHARLES (1991), 'A Society of Organizations', *Theory and Society*, 20: 725–62.

—— (1994), 'Pfeffer's Slips!', *Academy of Management Review*, 19/2: 191–4.

PFEFFER, JEFFREY (1993), 'Barriers to the Advance of Organizational Science: Paradigm Development as a Dependent Variable', *Academy of Management Review*, 18/4: 599–620.

PHILLIPS, NELSON (1995), 'Telling Organizational Tales: On the Role of Narrative Fiction in the Study of Organizations', *Organization Studies*, 16/4: 625–49.

POLKINGHORNE, DONALD (1987), *Narrative Knowing and the Human Sciences* (Albany, NY: State University of New York Press).

PONDY, LOUIS, FROST, PETER F., MORGAN, GARETH, and DANDRIDGE, THOMAS (1983) (eds.), *Organizational Symbolism* (Greenwich, Conn.: JAI Press).

PORTER, DENNIS (1981), *The Pursuit of Crime: Art and Ideology in Detective Fiction* (New Haven: Yale University Press).

PRED, ALLAN (1995), *Recognizing European Modernities: A Montage of the Present* (London: Routledge).

PROPP, VLADIMIR (1968), *Morphology of the Folktale* (Austin, Tex.: University of Texas Press).

PUTNAM, LINDA, AND PACANOWSKY, MICHAEL (1983) (eds.), *Communication in Organizations: An Interpretive Approach* (Beverly Hills, Calif.: Sage).

RICOEUR, PAUL (1981), 'The Model of the Text: Meaningful Action Considered as Text', in John B. Thompson (ed. and trans.), *Hermeneutics and the Human Sciences* (Cambridge: Cambridge University Press), 197–221.

—— (1984), *Time and Narrative*, i (Chicago: University of Chicago Press).

RIESSMAN, CATHERINE KOHLER (1993), *Narrative Analysis* (Newbury Park, Calif.: Sage).

RORTY, RICHARD (1980), *Philosophy and the Mirror of Nature* (Oxford: Basil Blackwell).

—— (1982), *Consequences of Pragmatism* (Minneapolis: University of Minnesota Press).

—— (1989), *Contingency, Irony and Solidarity* (Cambridge: Cambridge University Press).

—— (1991*a*), 'Inquiry as Recontextualization: An Anti-Dualist Account of Interpretation', in *Objectivity, Relativism and Truth*, I (New York: Cambridge University Press), 93–110.

—— (1991*b*), 'On Ethnocentrism: A Reply to Clifford Geertz', in *Objectivity, Relativism and Truth*, I (New York: Cambridge University Press), 203–10.

—— (1992*a*), 'Cosmopolitarianism without Emancipation: A Response to Lyotard', in Scott Lash and Jonathan Friedman (eds.), *Modernity and Identity* (Oxford: Blackwell), 59–72.

—— (1992*b*), 'The Pragmatist's Progress', in Umberto Eco, *Interpretation and Overinterpretation* (Cambridge: Cambridge University Press), 89–108.

ROWEN, NORMA (1991), 'The Detective in Search of the Lost Tongue of Adam: Paul Auster's *City of Glass*', *Critique*, 32/4: 224–34.

RUTHERFORD, J. D., and HEMMINGS, FREDRICK W. J. (1978), 'Realism in Spain and Portugal', in Fredrick W. J. Hemmings (ed.), *The Age of Realism* (Brighton: Harvester Press, 265–322.

SANDELANDS, LLOYD E. (1990), 'What is so Practical about Theory? Lewin Revisited', *Journal for the Theory of Social Behaviour*, 20/3: 235–62.

—— and DRAZIN, ROBERT (1989), 'On the Language of Organization Theory', *Organization Studies*, 10/4: 457–78.

SCHAFFER, SIMON (1993), 'Augustan Realities: Nature's Representatives and their Cultural Resources in the Early Eighteenth Century', in George Levine (ed.), *Realism and Representation: Essays on the Problem of Realism in Relation to Science, Literature, and Culture* (Madison: University of Wisconsin Press), 279–318.

SCHÖN, DONALD (1983), *The Reflective Practitioner* (New York: Basic Books).

SCHÜTZ, ALFRED (1973), 'On Multiple Realities', in *Collected Papers*, I. *The Problem of Social Reality* (The Hague: Martinus Nijhoff), 207–59.

SCOTT, JOAN (1986), 'Gender: A Useful Category of Historical Analysis', *American Historical Review*, 91: 1053–75.

SEBEOK, THOMAS A., and UMIKER-SEBEOK, JEAN (1983), ' "Voi conoscete il mio metodo": Un confronto fra Charles S. Peirce e Sherlock Holmes', in Umberto Eco and Thomas A. Sebeok (eds.), *Il segno dei tre: Holmes, Dupin, Peirce* (Milan: Bompianti), 27–64.

SELDEN, RAMAN (1985), *A Reader's Guide to Contemporary Literary Theory* (Brighton: Harvester Press).

SELZNICK, PHILIP (1949), *TVA and the Grass Roots: A Study in the Sociology of Formal Organizations* (Berkeley and Los Angeles: University of California Press).

SHAW, BERNARD (1971), *Collected Letters 1898–1910*, ed. Dan H. Laurence (New York: Viking).

SHENHAV, YEHOUDA (1999), *Manufacturing Rationality: The Engineering Foundations of the Managerial Revolution*, (Oxford: Oxford University Press).

SILVERMAN, DAVID (1971), *The Theory of Organizations* (New York: Basic Books).

—— (1993), *Interpreting Qualitative Data* (London: Sage).

—— and JONES, JILL (1976), *Organizational Work* (London: Collier Macmillan).

—— and TORODE, BRIAN (1980), *The Material Word: Some Theories About Language and Their Limits* (London: Routledge & Kegan Paul).

SIMMEL, GEORG (1902/1994), 'The Picture Frame', *Theory, Culture and Society*, 11: 11–17.

SIMS, DAVID, GABRIEL, YIANNIS, and FINEMAN, STEPHEN (1993), *Organizing and Organizations: An Introduction* (London: Sage).

SKRTIC, THOMAS M. (1985), 'Doing Naturalistic Research in Educational Organizations', in Yvonna S. Lincoln (ed.), *Organizational Theory and Inquiry: The Paradigm Revolution* (Beverly Hills, Calif.: Sage), 185–220.

SKÖLDBERG, KAJ (1994), 'Tales of Change: Public Administration Reform and Narrative Mode', *Organization Science*, 5/2: 219–38.

SMIRCICH, LINDA (1985), 'Is the Concept of Culture a Paradigm for Understanding Organizations and Ourselves?', in Peter J. Frost, Larry F. Moore, Mary R. Louis, Craig C. Lundberg, and Joanne Martin (eds.), *Organizational Culture* (Beverly Hills, Calif.: Sage), 3–72.

STEINER, GEORGE (1975/1992), *After Babel: Aspects of Language and Translation* (Oxford: Oxford University Press).

STEPHENSON, NEAL (1993), *Snow Crash* (New York: Bantam Books).

STERN, J. P. (1973), *On Realism* (London: Routledge & Kegan Paul).

STRANNEGÅRD, LARS (1998), *Green Ideas in Business* (Göteborg: BAS).

SYMONS, JULIAN (1992), 'A Postscript for the Nineties', a postscript to the 3rd edn. of *Bloody Murder* (1st edn., 1972; London: Pan Macmillan), 243–71.

SZYMBORSKA, WIESLAWA (1978), 'Slowka' (Words), *Literatura na Swiecie*, 1/81: 22–3.

THOMPSON, JAMES D. (1967), *Organizations in Action: Social Science Bases of Administrative Theory* (New York: McGraw-Hill).

THOMPSON, JON (1993), *Fiction, Crime and Empire: Clues to Modernity and Postmodernity* (Urbana, Ill.: University of Illinois Press).

TODOROV, TZVETAN (1977), *The Poetics of Prose* (Oxford: Blackwell).

—— (1990), *Genres in Discourse* (Cambridge: Cambridge University Press).

TRAWEEK, SHARON (1992), 'Border Crossings: Narrative Strategies in Science Studies and among Phycisists in Tsukuba Science City, Japan', in Andrew Pickering (ed.), *Science as Practice and Culture* (Chicago: University of Chicago Press).

TRUZZI, MARCELLO (1983), 'Sherlock Homes: Psicologo sociale applicato', in Umberto Eco and Thomas A. Sebeok (eds.), *Il segno dei tre: Holmes, Dupin, Peirce* (Milan: Bompianti), 65–94.

TURNER, BARRY (1990) (ed.), *Organisational Symbolism* (Berlin: de Gruyter).

TYLER, STEPHEN (1986), 'Post-Modern Ethnography: From Document of the Occult to Occult Document', in James Clifford and George E. Marcus (eds.), *Writing Culture: The Poetics and Politics of Ethnography* (Berkeley and Los Angeles: University of California Press), 122–40.

VAN MAANEN, JOHN (1988), *Tales of the Field* (Chicago: University of Chicago Press).

—— (1995a). 'Style as Theory', *Organization Science*, 6/1: 133–43.

—— (1995b). 'Fear and Loathing in Organization Studies', *Organization Science*, 6/6: 687–92.

VEBLEN, THORSTEN (1889/1994), *The Theory of the Leisure Class* (Mineola, NY: Dover Publications).

VEYNE, PAUL (1988), *Did the Greeks Believe in their Myths?* (Chicago: University of Chicago Press).

VICO, GIAMBATTISTA (1744/1960), *The New Science of Giambattista Vico* (Ithaca, NY: Cornell University Press).

WALDO, DWIGHT (1961), 'Organization Theory: An Elephantine Problem', *Public Administration Review*, 21: 210–25.

—— (1968), *The Novelist on Organization and Administration* (Berkeley and Los Angeles: Institute of Government Studies).

WATSON, TONY (1994), *In Search of Management* (London: Routledge).

Webster's New Collegiate Dictionary (1981) (Springfield, Mass.: G. & C. Merriam Company).

WATTS, CEDRIC (1990), *Literature and Money: Financial Myth and Literary Truth* (Hemel Hempstead: Harvester Wheatsheaf).

WEICK, KARL E. (1979), *The Social Psychology of Organizing* (Reading, Mass.: Addison-Wesley).

—— (1995), *Sensemaking in Organizations* (Thousands Oaks, Calif.: Sage).

WHITE, HAYDEN (1973), *Metahistory: The Historical Imagination in Nineteenth Century Europe* (Baltimore, Md.: Johns Hopkins University Press).

—— (1987), *The Content of the Form: Narrative Discourse and Historical Representation* (Baltimore, Md.: Johns Hopkins University Press).

WILLIAMSON, OLIVIER E. (1988) (ed.), *Organization Theory* (Oxford: Oxford University Press).

WILSON, ELISABETH (1991), *The Sphinx in the City* (London: Virago Press).

WINCH, PETER (1958), *The Idea of Social Science* (London: Routledge & Kegan Paul).

WITTGENSTEIN, L. (1953), *Philosophical Investigations* (Oxford: Oxford University Press).

WOLF, MARGERY (1992), *A Thrice-Told Tale: Feminism, Postmodernism, and Ethnographic Responsibility* (Stanford, Calif.: Stanford University Press).

WOLFF, ROLF (1998), 'Bortom miljömanagement', in Barbara Czarniawska (ed.), *Organisationsteori på svenska* (Malmö: Liber), 215–32.

WOOLGAR, STEVE (1988), *Science: The Very Idea* (London: Tavistock).

YANOW, DVORA (1996), *How Does a Policy Mean? Interpreting Policy and Organizational Actions* (Washington: Georgetown University Press).

INDEX